251 Essential
Drills for
Winning
Soccer

Michael G. Carpenter

PRENTICE HALL
Paramus, New Jersey 07652

This book is dedicated to my wife, Antonette,
and my four children, George, James, Amy and Katie,
whose love and support both enabled
and inspired me to complete it.

Library of Congress Cataloging-in-Publication Data

Carpenter, Michael G.
    251 essential drills for winning soccer / Michael G. Carpenter.
      p. cm.
    ISBN 0-13-040750-X (spiral wire)   ISBN 0-13-042587-7 (paper)
    1. Soccer—Training.   I. Title: Two hundred fifty-one essential drills for
winning soccer.   II. Title.

GV943.9.T7 C37 2001
796.334—dc21   00-065220

©2001 by Prentice Hall

Acquisitions Editor: *Connie Kallback*
Production Editor: *Jacqueline Roulette*
Interior Design/Formatting: *Robyn Beckerman*

Printed in the United States of America

10 9 8 7 6 5 4 3 2 1   *10 9 8 7 6 5 4 3 2 1*

ISBN 0-13-040750-X (spiral wire)   ISBN 0-13-042587-7 (paper)

PRENTICE HALL
Paramus, NJ 07652

http://www.phdirect.com

ABOUT THE AUTHOR

Michael Carpenter, a graduate of Boston University, has been coaching soccer on all levels—high school, middle school, and beginning players in recreational leagues—for nearly 20 years and is currently program director for Viking Soccer Camps in Massachusetts. A native of Great Britain, he began playing soccer at age three. He earned the honor of being a member of the England Public Schools National Team, representing all of England in the categories of Under 16 and Under 18, for three years before coming to the United States at age 22 on a Boston University soccer scholarship. At the university, he was named to the All-American Academic team and was also awarded the male student athlete award.

ABOUT THIS BOOK

Soccer is played by over 250 million people in almost every country in the world, making it, undoubtedly, the world's most popular sport. Many factors contribute to making soccer such an exciting sport to play, for example:

- The game is understood easily and requires very little equipment.

- Height and weight are not so important as in many other sports.

- Strength, stamina, flexibility and quick thinking are all achieved as a result of the exercise involved in playing the game no matter what the age or level of players involved.

- Children can begin to learn and play the game of soccer at a very young age.

- People of all ages can continue to play and enjoy it for many years.

Soccer is played at its best when played simply, which means that the most successful teams are those that strive to play the game using simple but effective skills. For example, a team that consists of players who pass the ball and then move to a space where they may be available to receive another pass will invariably do better than a team of players who individually try to dribble past all the opposing players and do not know how to pass even when they need to. Soccer players who can perform the essential skills outlined in this resource will do well in their present teams and will also have an invaluable set of tools at their disposal as they continue to practice and play.

As with any sport, it is important to learn good, sound fundamental techniques since bad habits can be very difficult to break. It is with this concept in mind that I have written this resource; all the skills, drills, and exercises are basic and described in very plain English for ultimate mastery by any soccer player. In addition, all the drills and exercises described have been carefully tested to ensure they will work and benefit players of a wide age range.

Organization of this resource

251 Essential Drills for Winning Soccer is organized into 12 sections for quick accessibility. You'll find the contents exceptionally easy to use, with most drills printed one per page and often accompanied by illustrations or diagrams to demonstrate form or process. Drill titles tell exactly what skill is to be practiced.

Each section addresses one essential skill or aspect of the game and begins with a brief introduction that describes the basic techniques for performing that skill. This is followed by a number of basic, as well as more advanced drills, aimed at practicing and improving that particular skill.

The first section includes 31 warm-up drills and 27 stretching drills. Most of these are quite brief and can be understood at a glance. Warm-ups and stretching are essential for players to avoid pulled muscles and injuries.

Kicking, one of the most essential soccer skills, is the focus of the second section. It explains a number of methods for kicking with the inside of the foot or the instep and features 18 passing drills, and 15 for shooting.

The 13 drills in Section 3 provide instruction and practice tips for trapping—stopping or slowing—the ball with the feet, thigh, chest, head, or any part of the body except hands or arms.

Using the 19 drills in Section 4, players will practice dribbling, one of the most fundamental elements of soccer. Developing this skill requires continued practice, regardless of the player's level.

The drills in Section 5 give players a chance to concentrate on tackling—using the feet to take the ball away from an opposing player. The actual tackle is described, step-by-step, along with practice tips in nine basic drills for using the front, block, or slide tackle. Emphasis is also placed on avoiding injury to other players.

Section 6 focuses on the throw-in—the only time players, other than the goalkeeper, can use their hands. Seven drills offer ways to practice stationary throw-ins and throw-ins with a run-up.

Thirteen drills in Section 7 give players practice in the basic method and principles of heading the ball, including jumping, flick heading to help the ball progress, and redirecting the ball.

Section 8 is a comprehensive study of goalkeeping, which supplies how-to descriptions and practice in stance; basic handling of the ball (ground shots, catching waist-high and chest-high balls, and catching balls above the head); positioning; coming off the goal line; diving saves; calling for the ball; and building the attack from the goalkeeper. A total of 19 drills are included.

Section 9 covers general tactics with an emphasis on keeping the play simple and includes a list of ten commonly used tactics that coaches instruct their teams to use. In addition to general tactics, it also features scrimmages, systems of play, and drills for positions of defender, attacker, and midfielder with a total of 32 drills.

Section 10 presents 43 quick fitness drills in a wide variety that helps you keep your players motivated.

Two final sections conclude this resource with a recap of soccer rules and suggestions for five easy-to-follow practice sessions, as well as blank practice session tables that you can copy as many times as needed to create practice sessions for your team.

Recommendations for equipment

Be sure that any necessary equipment items—such as cones, goals, and balls—are present at all practices. A set of colored nylon vests are a very good investment, since they not only enable players to clearly distinguish their teammates from opponents during practice sessions, but they also come on and off quickly so that teams can be altered whenever necessary.

Shinguards are essential for all players, whether competing in a game or practicing. Soccer players will get kicked in the shins many times during their soccer playing days, and shinguards can prevent both serious shin injuries and minor but painful bruises. While many people will disagree, it is extremely important to wear shinguards during practice sessions, since kicks to the shin are accidental and do not happen only in real game situations.

Players improve by kicking soccer balls and by performing skills and drills with the ball. For this reason, it is important to have enough soccer balls at practice sessions for every player to have his or her own ball.

Keeping instruction clear and simple

Because players will learn best by actually practicing, keep verbal teaching and advice as understandable and short as possible. Remember also that different players have different abilities. This is especially so with children, but even with other players, who often learn at very different rates. Introduce the simple aspects of a drill first, have the players try to perform the drill, and then develop it further when they have clearly mastered the basics. If a drill is not working, modify it or switch it to something else; perhaps it was too advanced or the players simply didn't understand it the first time through. The next time you try the drill, explain it again and carry it out differently to make sure it works. You may also want to take advantage of the book's design as a "reproducible resource," and copy individual drills for players or assistant coaches.

You'll find practices to be more effective and organized if you take the time to prepare in advance. This book will help you do that by giving a clear idea of what you need to teach and practice at a particular session.

Ultimately, the goal of this resource is to help you provide your players with a wide variety of drills and games to further develop their skills for playing soccer—and have some fun as they practice.

CONTENTS

Section 1

WARMING UP AND STRETCHING

WARM-UP DRILLS

STRETCHING DRILLS

Section 2

KICKING (PASSING AND SHOOTING)

PASSING DRILLS

SHOOTING DRILLS

Section 3

TRAPPING

TRAPPING DRILLS

Section 4

DRIBBLING

DRIBBLING DRILLS

Section 5
TACKLING

TACKLING DRILLS

Section 6
THROW-INS

THROW-IN DRILLS

Section 7
HEADING

HEADING DRILLS

GOALKEEPING

GOALKEEPING DRILLS

TACTICS AND POSITIONS

TACTICAL AND POSITIONAL DRILLS

Section 10

FITNESS DRILLS

Section 11

THE RULES OF SOCCER

Section 12

FIVE EASY-TO-FOLLOW PRACTICE SESSIONS

KEY FOR DIAGRAM AND FIGURES

Pass/Shot o------->

Player moving with the ball o o o o o o →

Player moving without the ball ———————→

Header ♀ ♀ ♀ ♀ ♀ ♀ →

Throw × × × × × × →

Volley ∗ ∗ ∗ ∗ ∗ ∗ →

<u>Players:</u> defender △

attacker ☐

goalkeeper ⬡

player (general) X Y Z 1 2 3 A B C, etc.

Player's new positions after moving from original position:

defender △ (dashed)

attacker ☐ (dashed)

goalkeeper ⬡ (dashed)

Coach ▯

Cones Λ

Soccer ball ○

Tackle ⊗

©2001 by Prentice Hall

Section 1

WARMING UP AND STRETCHING

Section 1
WARMING UP AND STRETCHING

Playing the game of soccer helps players build speed, stamina, flexibility, and suppleness, and also helps keep body weight at a good level. Although stretching is often considered only necessary for teenagers and adults, basic warm-ups and stretches will do children no harm. It is a good idea to have young players as well as older ones become accustomed to warming up and stretching since, as they get older, it becomes increasingly important for them to do so in order to avoid pulled muscles and other injuries.

Warm-ups and stretches can be performed with or without a soccer ball, but it is recommended the ball be used whenever possible in order to prevent boredom and, more important, because players benefit greatly from touching a soccer ball as much as possible. The following list of warm-ups and stretches can be performed in any order, but it is recommended that the more gentle ones (the first ones in the list) be performed first. It is also very important that players jog at the start of the warm-up and stretching sessions so the heart rate rises and blood is pumping quicker to the various muscles that are to be stretched and loosened. Warm-up and stretching drills are often performed together, whereby players jog for a certain distance, stop to stretch, jog some more, stop to stretch some more, and so on.

WARM-UP DRILLS

1. JUGGLING THE BALL

This refers to keeping the ball in the air with the feet, thighs, and head. Juggling is an excellent warm-up drill since it gets cold and stiff muscles moving and warmed, offers an excellent means of practicing close ball skill (with the weaker and stronger foot) and is great for building confidence for handling the ball. Many of the great soccer stars spend hours juggling on their own and with teammates, since it is a skill that can always be improved upon.

Players who have never juggled a soccer ball before may find this skill very difficult at first, and should learn to juggle by allowing the ball to drop from their hands to the floor, bounce once, and then kick it back to their hands.

Progress can then be made by

- kicking it twice or more before catching it,

- using the thighs to juggle as well,

- dropping it directly to the feet with no bounce first, and

- eventually not using the hands at all.

Many players will not be able to complete more than one or two juggles; however, they should not be discouraged since it will still be beneficial for them. They will begin to enjoy the exercise greatly as they see their number of juggles and skill handling of the ball slowly increase.

2. JOGGING

Players should jog at least one or two laps of the field before exercising to ensure the heart rate rises and the blood is pumping to the various muscles being stretched and used to play soccer.

3. WINDMILL

Players either jog along or stand still while they swing their arms around in a windmill-like movement. Both arms should be swung forward, then both arms backward, and then one backward and the other forward at the same time, if possible.

4. HAND CLAP

Players either jog or stand still while they clap their hands, first with arms extended in front of the body, and then with arms swung back and extended to clap hands behind the back, and so on.

5. JOG AND PASS

Two players stand about 10 yards apart and jog up and down the field passing the ball to one another.

6. KNEES UP

Players jog forward using quick short steps, while exaggerating the height to which they bring their knees up with each step.

7. HEEL TO HAND

Players jog along while at the same time exaggerating the height to which they bring their heels back, so they kick their hands—which are held behind them—with the heel of the foot with each step.

8. JOG AND BEND

Players jog along in a straight line while bending their knees every three or four yards to touch the ground either with the left hand, the right hand, or both hands.

9. HEAD ROTATION

Players stand still and rotate their heads around and around, and up and down. The rotation should be performed in both directions.

10. JOGGING FORWARD AND BACKWARD

Players jog along in a straight line. When the coach blows the whistle, the players turn and jog backward. When the coach blows the whistle again, the players turn and jog forward again, and so on.

11. HAND KICK

Players jog forward in a straight line. Every three or four yards, players kick the left foot up as high as possible to touch the right hand which is held out in front of them and then perform the same action with the right foot kicking the left hand after three or four more yards have been covered.

12. JOG AND SPRINT

Players jog along in a straight line. When the coach blows the whistle, players jog faster. When the coach blows the whistle again, players sprint. When the coach blows the whistle again, players jog slowly again. (The time period between the whistle blows should be only a few seconds, since this exercise is designed as a warm-up drill and not a fitness drill in which players would be expected to run farther and faster.)

13. SHUTTLES

Players line up behind a cone with three more cones 5 or 10 yards apart in a line in front of them. The first player runs from the first cone to the second cone and back to the first cone, then to the third cone and back to the first cone, then to the fourth cone and back to the first cone before the next player performs the same drill.

14. RUNNING PLUS

Players line up behind one cone, with another cone 5 or 10 yards in front of them. The first player runs to the cone 10 yards away, performs 10 push-ups (or sit-ups, star-jumps, or squat-thrusts), and then runs back to the start to tag the next person who performs the same routine.

15. FORWARD AND BACKWARD SPRINT

Players line up behind one cone with another cone 5 or 10 yards in front of them. The front player sprints forward to the cone 10 yards away and then sprints backward to the start, and tags the next player.

16. RUN AND SIT

Players run forward. Each time the coach blows the whistle, players must sit down, get up again as quickly as possible, and resume running.

17. SIDEWAYS STRIDES

Players move along sideways by taking large spring jump strides so the leading leg and back leg meet between each stride. Players should turn 180 degrees every three or four strides so they are facing the opposite direction and the leading leg changes.

18. SIDEWAYS SWIVEL

Players move along sideways while first twisting the body to the right and stepping the left leg over the right leg, and then twisting the body to the left and stepping the right leg over the left leg. Players should turn 180 degrees every three or four steps.

19. LEG CROSS

Players jog along in a straight line by crossing the left leg in front of and across the right leg, and then crossing the right leg in front of and across the left leg, and so on.

20. LEG OUT

Players jog along in a straight line by stepping the left leg forward and out to the left and then the right leg forward and out to the right, and so on.

21. LEAP STEP

Players move ahead by taking a giant leap-step forward and to the right with the right foot, and then a giant leap-step forward and to the left with the left foot, and so on.

22. SKIP AND TWIST

Players skip along in a straight line while twisting the upper body and arms in one direction and the legs and lower body in the opposite direction at the same time. Players twist from one side to the other after each skip.

23. JOG AND JUMP

Players jog and jump in the air every three or four yards to head an imaginary soccer ball. Players should alternate heading straight on, to the left, and to the right.

24. SKIP WITH KNEES HIGH

Players skip along in a straight line exaggerating the height of each knee as it is brought up with each successive step, so the knee almost touches the chest.

25. KNEE LIFT

Players jog along in a straight line at a very slow pace. Every three or four yards each player lifts a knee to waist height in front of the body, and then turns the leg and foot outward to the side, alternating the leg each three or four yards.

26. TURN AND LIFT THE KNEE

Players jog along slowly in a straight line. Every three or four yards players turn slightly toward one side; lift the knee of the leg on that side about waist high; and turn and move the knee, leg, body, and foot inward; and then back to the floor. After three or four more yards the player turns slightly towards the other side and performs the same movement using the other leg.

27. JUMP FORWARD AND BACKWARD

Players move forward 10 yards by jumping with both feet together and then backward 10 yards by jumping in the same manner.

28. ROTATION

Players stand with legs apart and hands on hips so that they can rotate their bodies around and around. Players should perform this rotation in both directions.

29. BEND AND JUMP

Players jog along and at every three or four yards, bend their knees, touching the ground and then jumping to head an imaginary soccer ball. Players should alternate heading straight on, to the left and to the right.

30. AROUND THE BODY

Players jog along carrying a soccer ball, which they pass around the back of the body from one hand to the other.

31. UNDER THE LEG

Players jog along carrying a soccer ball, which they pass from one hand to the other under one leg and then under the other leg, and so on.

STRETCHING DRILLS

Players should take time to stretch both before and after practice sessions and games. Each stretch should be performed for at least 10 seconds (preferably more), and players should not bounce or jerk during any stretch.

32. BALANCING ON ONE LEG

Players stand on one leg and bring the other leg up behind them with the knee pointing down. The elevated foot is held behind the back. If players find it difficult to balance on one leg, this drill can be performed in pairs, whereby the two players stand together and each holds on to the other's shoulder with the spare hand to maintain balance. Balance is a very important part of soccer and players should be encouraged to perform this exercise on their own; players will find that it is easier to maintain balance if they keep their free arm—the one not holding the foot behind the back— vertically downward, and also if they look downward, focusing on something on the ground.

33. REACH FOR YOUR ANKLES

Players stand with legs wide apart. Players first attempt to reach and hold the left ankle with the right hand, then the right ankle with the left hand, and then the left ankle with the left hand and the right ankle with the right hand at the same time.

34. ONE LEG UP

Players stand with legs apart—one in front of the other. The feet, body, and head should be turned to one side. Players now bend the front knee so it is also pointing forward, while keeping the back leg straight and lifting it, and keeping the upper body upright. The straight leg should almost be touching the floor. Players change directions after 10 or 20 seconds so that the back leg now becomes the front leg.

35. LEAN AND LIFT

Players stand with legs wide apart. Players first lean to the left while bending the left knee and keeping the right leg straight, then to the right while bending the right knee and keeping the left leg straight.

36. SQUAT AND PUSH

Players crouch down to the squatting position, put their hands on the tops of their feet, and push their legs as far apart as possible using their elbows and forearms.

37. SPREAD AND SWING

Players stand with their legs wide apart and quickly swing the left arm to the right foot, the right arm to the left foot and so on. Both arms and legs should be kept straight at all times.

38. UPPER BODY TWIST

Players stand with feet about shoulder's width apart and turn the upper body as far in one direction as possible so they are looking behind them. They then turn the upper body as far as possible in the other direction.

39. LEAN SIDEWAYS

Players stand with legs about shoulder's width apart and hands on hips. Players then lean sideways as far as they can in one direction before doing the same in the other direction.

40. TOUCH YOUR TOES

Players stand with legs together and straight while they lean forward and attempt to reach down to touch their toes. If some players find they can easily reach their toes, they should attempt to touch the back of their heels, still ensuring that the legs remain absolutely straight.

41. LEGS CROSSED AND TOES TOUCHED

Players stand with the left leg crossed over the right leg with legs together and straight while they lean forward and attempt to touch their toes. Players then cross the right leg over the left leg and perform the same stretch to touch the toes. If players find that they can easily reach their toes, they should attempt to reach the back of the heels.

42. SIT AND TOUCH YOUR TOES

Players sit on the floor with their legs together and straight in front of them. Players attempt to use both hands to touch and hold their toes.

43. ROLL AROUND

Players stand with their legs together and, using their hands, roll a soccer ball in circles around their legs. The ball should be rolled around in a clockwise as well as in a counterclockwise direction.

44. ROLLING FIGURE EIGHT

Players stand with their legs apart and, using their hands, roll a soccer ball through and around their legs in a figure-eight pattern. The ball should be rolled around in a clockwise as well as in a counterclockwise direction.

45. PASSING PAIRS

Players stand back-to-back in pairs with one soccer ball for each duo. One player starts by holding the ball in the hands and passing it to the partner's hands behind and to one side. The players then exchange the ball again by turning the bodies and hands to the opposite side as quickly as possible, and so on.

46. OVER AND UNDER

Players stand back-to-back in pairs with one soccer ball for each pair. They must stand with legs open. One player starts with the ball and hands it to the partner by passing the ball over the back of the head. The partner receives the ball above the head and passes it back to the other player through the legs, and so on.

47. LEAVE AND RETRIEVE

Players sit on the ground while holding a ball. They turn as far as they can to one side, put the ball down behind themselves, leave it there, and then turn in the other direction to pick up the ball before performing the movement again. This drill should be performed so that the ball is left first for a number of times on one side and then for a number of times on the other side.

48. ANKLE SWIRLS

Players stand balanced on one foot while they extend the other leg slightly out in front of them and rotate the ankle and foot of the extended leg. The rotation should be performed in both directions.

49. LEAN AND SLIDE

Players stand with their legs about shoulder's width apart and their arms by their sides. Players lean first to the left while sliding the left hand and arm as far down the left side of the body as possible, and then to the right while sliding the right hand and arm as far down the right side of the body as possible.

50. LIE DOWN AND TOUCH YOUR TOES

Players lie flat on their backs with the left leg straight out on the floor and the right leg lifted upward. Players then attempt to hold the toes of the right foot, while ensuring that this leg remains straight. The right leg is then placed straight out along the floor while the left leg is positioned vertically upward, so that the player can attempt to hold the toes of the left foot.

51. FOOT BACK

Players sit on the floor with the left leg straight out in front of them and the right leg bent at the knee so that the right foot is on the ground behind and to the right of the body. The right leg is then placed straight out in front of the body and the left leg bent at the knee and pulled back so that it is on the ground behind and to the left of the body.

52. HEAD TO TOES

Players sit down and bring both feet up toward the body so that the soles of the feet are touching. Players now hold the feet as they try to move their head as close to the feet as possible.

53. PUSH DOWN WITH THE ELBOWS

Players sit down and bring both feet up toward the body so that the soles of the feet are touching. Players now hold the feet and push the elbows against the knees in order to push the legs as far down toward the ground as possible.

54. PUSH IN WITH THE ELBOWS

Players sit on the floor with the left leg straight out in front of them, and the right leg (with the knee raised) and right foot placed across to the left side of the left leg. The upper body is then turned toward the right and the left elbow pushed against the outside of the right knee so as to push the right leg further toward the left.

The same exercise is then performed by placing the right leg straight out in front of the body and placing the left leg (with the knee raised) and left foot across to the right side of the right leg. The upper body is then turned toward the left and the right elbow used to push against the outside of the left knee in order to push the left leg further to the right.

55. LEGS SPREAD, TOES TOUCHED

Players sit on the floor with legs straight and spread as far apart as possible. Players attempt to touch the right hand to the left toes, then the left hand to the right toes, and finally both the left hand to the left toes and the right hand to the right toes simultaneously.

56. AROUND THE FEET AND BACK

Players sit on the ground with legs together and straight out in front of them. They then roll a soccer ball in a circular motion around their feet and around their back. This drill should be carried out in both a clockwise and in a counterclockwise direction.

57. LIFTING WITH THE FEET

Players lie on their backs flat on the floor with a soccer ball between the feet. Players lift the ball with the feet and place it on the ground behind the head. They then pick the ball up with the hands, put it back between the feet and perform the exercise again.

58. KICKING WHILE SUPINE

Players lie on the floor on their backs. Players take the ball in their hands and hold it on the floor at arm's length to the left of the body so that they can bring the right foot up to kick the ball while still holding onto it. They then move the ball across to the right side of the body and kick it with the left foot.

©2001 by Prentice Hall

59. BEND UP

Players lie on the floor on their backs and bring the legs up and over the head so the toes are touching the ground by the shoulders and ears.

Section 2

KICKING

(PASSING AND SHOOTING)

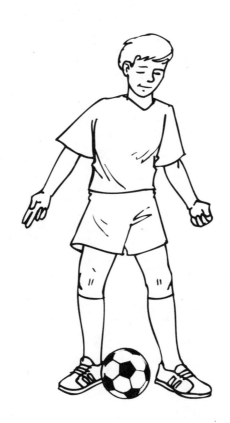

PRESTON RIDGE CAMPUS

Section 2

KICKING (PASSING AND SHOOTING)

Since soccer is a game played almost entirely by using your feet (except goalkeepers who may use their hands), it is obvious that kicking the ball correctly is of prime importance to anyone who wishes to learn and play the sport at any level.

Kicking with the inside of the foot

Kicking with the inside of the foot involves the part of the foot from the big toe to the ankle. This method promotes very accurate short passes and shots.

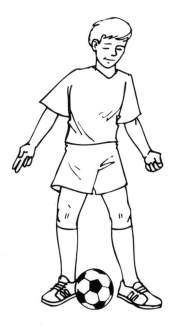

METHOD

- Place the non-kicking foot alongside the ball in the direction that the ball is intended to go.

- Turn the kicking foot outward so that it is at 90 degrees to the planted non-kicking foot.

- Keep the eyes on the ball and swing the kicking foot back and then through the ball, with the ankle locked, striking the ball at the midpoint, and following through the ball with the foot and leg, moving in the direction that the player wishes the ball to go.

A low hard pass is performed by placing the body weight and head over the ball, while a lofted pass is performed by leaning back slightly.

©2001 by Prentice Hall

Kicking with the instep

The instep is the part of the foot that is most commonly used to kick the ball since it produces powerful and long kicks. This method can be used for shooting, long clearances, long passes, free kicks and corner kicks. The instep refers to the area from the big toe up to the shoe laces. The power is a result of the swing before, the follow through after kicking the ball, and the speed at which the foot strikes the ball.

METHOD

- Keep the eyes firmly fixed on ball when kicking it.
- Approach the ball from a slight angle.
- Place the non-kicking foot about eight inches to the side of the ball. At the same time the kicking foot, with ankle locked, comes forward from its back-swing and strikes the ball with the instep.
- The toes of the kicking foot should be pointed down as the foot strikes the ball.
- Place the non-kicking foot in the direction the ball is intended to go.
- Follow through with the kicking foot in the direction the player wishes the ball to go.

To kick the ball low and hard, the head and body weight must be kept over the ball, and the ball must be struck at the midpoint. In order to lift the ball, the player must strike it below the midpoint, lean the head and body slightly back, and position the non-kicking foot slightly behind the ball. The ball is usually struck low and hard when shooting on goal, since a shot of this nature is more difficult for a goalkeeper to save. The ball is usually lifted into the air for a long pass, a corner kick, or a free kick.

PASSING DRILLS

60. BASIC PASSING WITH THE INSIDE OF THE FOOT

Organization:

Two players stand between 5 and 10 yards apart with one ball.

Purpose:

To practice accurate short passing to a teammate

Procedure:

Players pass the ball to each other with the inside of the foot, control it, and pass it back. Enough weight should be put on the ball so the pass is firm enough to reach the teammate before an opponent can intercept it, but the pass must be neither too soft so it does not reach the teammate nor too hard so the teammate has difficulty controlling the ball.

Coaching points:

Coaches must ensure that players watch the ball as they strike it, since lifting the head at the moment of contact is a common error, which causes the ball to be miss-hit and go away from the intended target. Players must **not** use their toes to kick the ball. Players **must** be instructed to perform this exercise with the weaker as well as the preferred stronger foot.

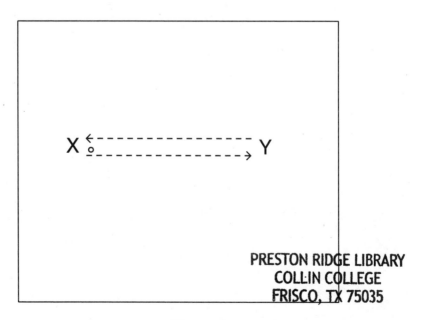

61. QUICK AND ACCURATE PASSING

Organization:
All players form a circle around a player in the middle.

Purpose:
To practice quick short passes

Procedure:
One of the players making up the circle starts with the ball and passes it to the player in the middle. This player controls the ball and passes it back to the next player, either in a clockwise or counterclockwise direction. The drill continues until the ball arrives back at the first player.

Coaching points:
All players should call for the ball each time they wish to receive it and should concentrate on making accurate, well-weighted passes.

©2001 by Prentice Hall

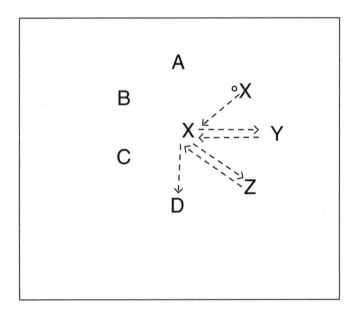

62. ACCURACY PASSING

Organization:

Two players stand about 10 to 15 yards apart and practice kicking the ball to each other between two cones positioned halfway between them.

Purpose:

To pass accurately kicking with the inside of the foot

Procedure:

As players improve, the cones can be positioned closer together and the players can stand farther apart. Players should practice using both feet to kick the ball. This drill could also be carried out by having a player in the middle with legs open in place of the cones.

Coaching points:

The non-kicking foot must be placed alongside the ball facing the direction of the cones. The kicking foot is turned outward at 90 degrees to the non-kicking foot, and after kicking the ball, the kicking foot and leg follow through in the direction of the cones. Players must watch the ball as they kick it, and keep head and body weight over the ball to ensure it stays on the ground after it is kicked.

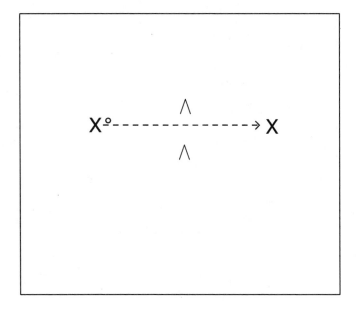

63. SOCCER GOLF (ACCURACY PASSING)

Organization:

Position a number of cones at different points on the soccer field representing the various holes of a golf course.

Purpose:

To practice accuracy passing with a game that's fun

Procedure:

Each player has his or her own ball and counts the number of kicks it takes to reach and touch each hole (cone). The player who takes the least number of kicks wins, just as in golf.

Coaching points:

Both the accuracy and the weight of passes become important so players do not kick the ball way past the cone they're trying to hit.

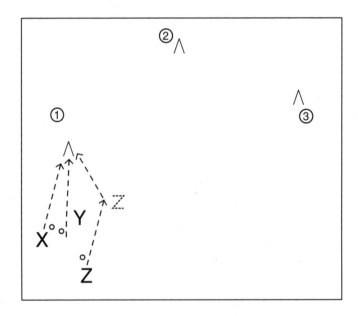

64. SOCCER TENNIS

Organization:

Pair up players on an imaginary mini tennis court with no net (see diagram below).

Purpose:

To practice one-touch passing

Procedure:

Players pass the ball across the line to each other using one-touch passing and keeping the ball in bounds.

Coaching points:

One-touch passes must not be kicked too hard since the receiver must be able to control and pass the ball back in one movement. They must also not be too soft; otherwise, the pass will not reach the teammate.

NOTE: Although players in the diagram are shown as defender and attacker, all players, regardless of position, should practice this drill.

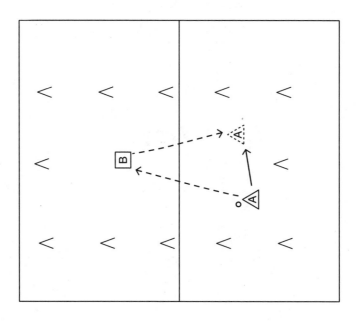

65. SOCCER VOLLEYBALL

Organization:
Pair up players on an imaginary volleyball court with no net (see diagram below).

Purpose:
To practice controlled volley passes

Procedure:
Players must keep the ball in the air as they pass the ball to each other over the line with one-touch passing.

Coaching points:
Passes must be perfectly weighted. Players should also use their heads and thighs to control and pass the ball.

NOTE: Although players in the diagram are shown as defender and attacker, all players, regardless of position, should practice this drill.

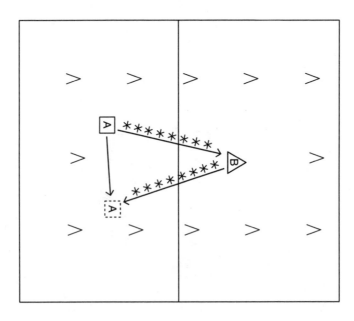

66. ONE-TOUCH PASSING WITH A TWIST

Organization:
Stand two players between 5 and 10 yards apart with one ball.

Purpose:
To practice accurate short one-touch passing to a teammate

Procedure:
The players pass the ball to each other, kicking with the inside of the foot and using one-touch passes. After each pass, players must turn 360 degrees and get ready for the next pass.

Coaching points:
Coaches must ensure players watch the ball as they strike it, since lifting the head at the moment of contact is a common error that causes the ball to be miss-hit and miss the intended target. One-touch passes must be well weighted. Players **must** be instructed to perform this exercise with their weaker as well as their stronger foot. Players should move to meet the ball.

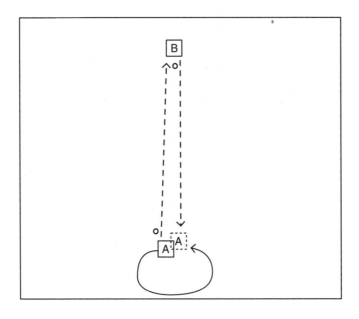

67. MOVING TO THE BALL

Organization:

Stand two players about 10 to 15 yards apart and have them kick the ball to each other.

Purpose:

To learn to move to the ball

Procedure:

Players must move quickly to the ball and not wait for it to arrive.

Coaching points:

Players must move to meet the ball as it is coming toward them, just as they would in a real game.

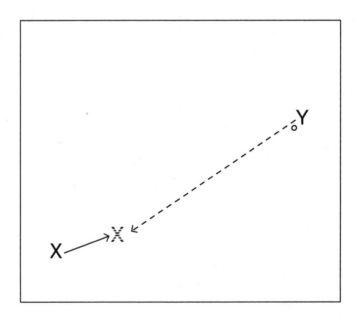

68. FIRST-TOUCH PASSING

Organization:

Stand two players about 10 to 15 yards apart and have them kick the ball to each other.

Purpose:

To meet the ball and make a quick first-time pass

Procedure:

As players pass the ball to each other, they must use only one touch/kick to return it.

Coaching points:

It now becomes even more important to watch the ball as it is kicked, since the ball can often pass over an uneven piece of ground and take a bounce up or movement sideways as it comes toward the receiver. Players must also weight the pass correctly so the receiving player is able to control and pass the ball in one movement; obviously it will be difficult to do this with a very hard pass.

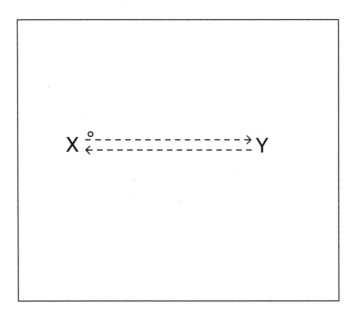

69. PASSING AND COMMUNICATING

Organization:

Players form a circle, with one ball used for the whole group.

Purpose:

To practice accuracy in passing and communicating between teammates

Procedure:

The player who starts with the ball calls out another's name and passes the ball to that player. The second player controls the ball and calls out another player's name and passes the ball to him or her, and so on.

Coaching points:

Players should plan who they will pass the ball to next as the ball is arriving. As players improve at this drill, it should be performed using one-touch passing.

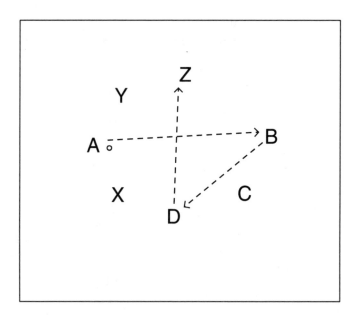

70. FOLLOW THE PASS

Organization:
Players form a circle, with one ball used for the whole group.

Purpose:
To practice moving after the pass is made

Procedure:
The player who starts with the ball calls out another player's name and passes the ball to that player. As soon as the pass is made, the player making the pass follows the pass and takes up the position where the receiver of the pass was standing. Meanwhile the receiver of the pass will have controlled the ball, called out another player's name, passed the ball to that player, and so on.

Coaching points:
As players improve at this drill, it should be performed using one-touch passing.

Variation:
Two balls are used. This means that the calling for the ball must now be very clear and decisive, and players must look up and be aware of the player and the ball moving around at the same time.

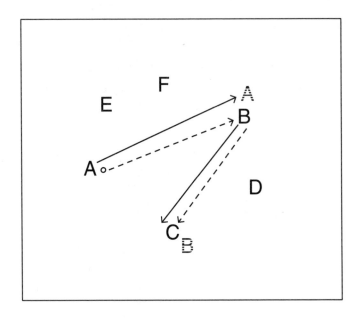

71. PASS AND MOVE QUICKLY TO MEET ANOTHER PASS

Organization:

Two players face each other about 10 yards apart, with a third player between them.

Purpose:

To practice moving to the ball to meet the pass

Procedure:

One of the outside players passes the ball to the player in the middle who controls the ball and quickly turns to pass the ball to the opposite outside player. This outside player controls the ball and passes it back to the player in the middle who again controls it and turns to pass it to the opposite outside player.

Coaching points:

The player in the middle must move to meet the ball, control it with one foot, and turn to pass it with the other foot as quickly as possible.

©2001 by Prentice Hall

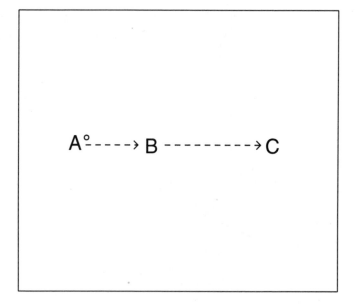

72. MOVE TO THE BALL, CONTROL AND PASS IT BACK, AND MOVE OFF FOR ANOTHER PASS

Organization:

Two players face each other about 10 yards apart with a ball each and with a third player between them.

Purpose:

To move quickly toward the ball to receive a pass

Procedure:

The player in the middle receives the pass and controls and kicks the ball back to the same player who served the ball before turning to move toward the other server to receive another pass.

Coaching points:

Moving to meet the ball as well as the control and pass should all be performed quickly.

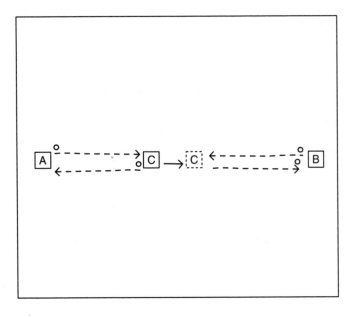

73. FIVE VERSUS TWO IN A CIRCLE

Organization:

Five players form a circle around two players.

Purpose:

To pass the ball in order to keep possession

Procedure:

The five players must pass the ball among themselves while keeping a circle formation. The two players in the middle must try to tackle the ball or win it by intercepting passes. If a player is tackled or if a bad pass leads to the ball traveling outside of the circle the tackled player or bad pass maker switches with one of the players in the middle.

Coaching points:

The players on the outside must control and pass the ball quickly. As players improve at this drill, they should play two-touch/one-touch passes. Obviously this same drill can be adapted to four versus one, seven versus three, etc. This drill is an excellent warm-up exercise for use at the start of a practice session or before a game, since players are practicing their passing, controlling, tackling, calling, and moving toward the ball. Players should also use the outside of the foot to pass the ball in this drill, since this method can be very effective at confusing the opponent as to where the ball is being kicked.

©2001 by Prentice Hall

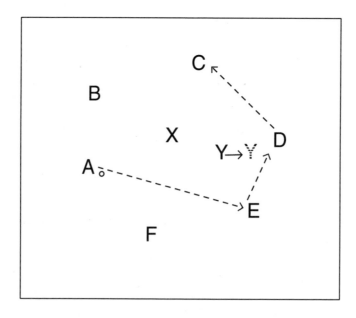

74. FIVE VERSUS TWO INSIDE A GRID

Organization:

Five versus two players.

Purpose:

To pass the ball in order to keep possession

Procedure:

All players can move anywhere inside the grid. The team with more players should be able to keep possession of the ball.

Coaching points:

The team with more players should be able to keep possession of the ball, but players must constantly move into free space and give the player with the ball good passing angles. A good passing angle means the player with the ball can pass the ball directly to other players who are positioned to the sides or in front of opponents and not behind them, where they obviously cannot receive a pass. This is often referred to as creating triangles, whereby players always support the player on the ball by giving him or her at least two passing options (so that the player with the ball and the two supporting players form a triangle).

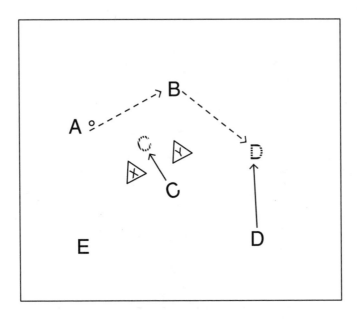

75. SEQUENTIAL PASSING

Organization:

Players are each given a number from one to eight (or one to however many players are participating).

Purpose:

To encourage players to support their teammates and to use good vision

Procedure:

Player one starts with the ball, and passes to player two, who passes to player three, and so on, until player eight receives the ball from player seven and passes it back to player one. After receiving and passing the ball, players must move to a different area where they see space, so all players are constantly moving.

Coaching points:

Players must support the player from whom they are going to receive the pass, as well as being aware of the player to whom they will pass to when they receive the ball. This requires good calling and vision; as the ball is coming toward them, players receiving the ball must look to see where the player who they will pass the ball to is positioned or is moving to. The player who they will be passing the ball to will help by calling for the ball and achieving a good position in which to receive the pass. Players passing the ball must also make good passes into the path of the moving receiver.

©2001 by Prentice Hall

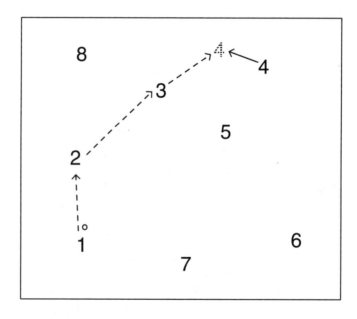

76. LONG PASSES

Organization:

Two players stand 15 to 40 yards away from two other players.

Purpose:

To practice long accurate passes

Procedure:

Player A kicks a long pass to player C, who controls the ball and lays it off to player D, who kicks a long pass to player A, who controls the ball and lays it off for player B to kick to player D, and so on. The long pass can be kicked using the instep, the inside of the foot, the volley, or another kicking method that the player wishes to practice. Players should also practice using both feet.

Coaching points:

Players receiving the ball should come to meet it, control it, and pass it off as quickly as possible. Although the long passes must be accurate, the drill should be carried out as quickly as possible just as in a real game.

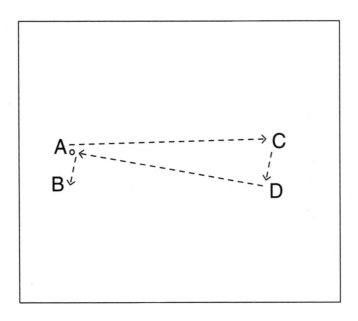

77. SUPPORTING TEAMMATES TO RECEIVE PASSES

Organization:
Set up several small goals (about two yards wide) using cones at various parts of the field. Using about half of the soccer field, set up a 10 on 10.

Purpose:
To encourage players to support each other and pass

Procedure:
Either team may score in any goal by passing the ball between the cones/goal to a teammate who receives it at the other side. Players must use vision in this drill to mark players, to see the opposing team's change of plays, to switch the play for their own team by passing long balls to players who are free in space, and by supporting the play.

Coaching points:
Players must read the game quickly in this drill so they support their players when their team is in possession of the ball, and mark all opponents and goals that they are defending when the ball is in the possession of the opposing team.

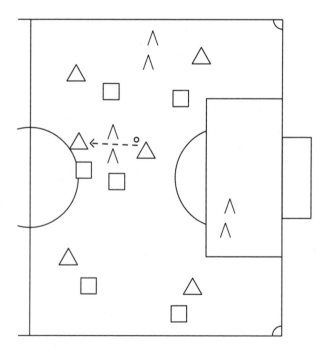

78. TEN PASSES EQUAL A GOAL

Organization:
A regular game is played except there are no goals or goalkeepers.

Purpose:
To encourage players to support their teammates and give them good passing angles

Procedure:
Each team must put together 10 (or fewer) consecutive passes to score a goal. Neither team is defending or attacking a goal because there are no goals or goalkeepers; the drill is all about possession.

Coaching points:
Players must always support the player with the ball so as to give him or her passing options. This involves supporting other players not only by players positioning themselves at an angle so the ball can be passed to them, but also by finding space in which the ball can be passed. If the play becomes bunched up, players must be able to use their vision to look for and find long passing opportunities, and teammates must think to find space to receive these long passes. (Obviously this drill can be changed to four, five, etc., consecutive passes equaling a goal.)

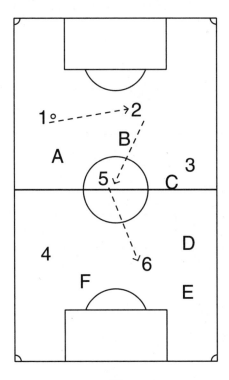

SHOOTING DRILLS

79. SHOOTING A STATIONARY BALL ON GOAL

Organization:

Players line up around the penalty box (each with a ball) and face the goal and goal-keeper.

Purpose:

To practice shooting the ball on goal from outside the penalty box

Procedure:

The player on one end of the line begins by shooting the ball. As soon as the goal-keeper has saved or attempted to save the ball, the next player shoots, and so on.

Coaching points:

Players should shoot the ball with the instep of the foot for more powerful shots, and with the inside of the foot for more accurate shots. Whichever method is used, players must watch the ball as they strike it, and should keep their head and weight over the ball to keep the ball low.

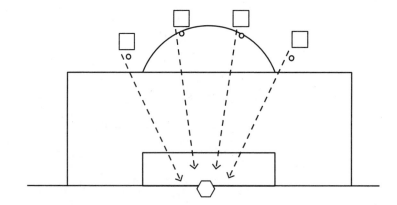

80. SHOOTING SEVERAL STATIONARY BALLS ON GOAL

Organization:

One player stands by a cone near the penalty box with many balls and faces the goal and goalkeeper.

Purpose:

To practice shooting the ball on goal from outside the penalty box

Procedure:

The player must run back and around the cone between each shot.

Coaching points:

Players should shoot the ball with the instep of the foot for more powerful shots, and with the inside of the foot for more accurate shots. Whichever method is used, players must watch the ball as they strike it, and should keep their head and weight over the ball to keep the ball low. Players must remember to shoot the ball low and hard toward a corner of the goal so their shots are as difficult as possible for the goalkeeper to save.

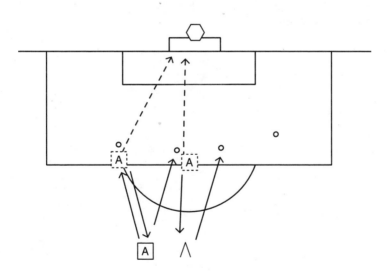

81. WALL PASS AND SHOOT

Organization:

The player with the ball passes the ball to a teammate, runs past the defender to receive a return pass, and then shoots on goal.

Purpose:

To practice shooting a moving ball

Procedure:

Player A, who is at the front of the line, runs toward the defender (player B), and passes the ball to a teammate (player C) before arriving at the defender. Player A then runs past player B and receives a return pass from player C, which must be shot on goal as quickly as possible (preferably a first-time shot).

Coaching points:

Players must perform this drill quickly, since in a game they will usually have very little time in front of the goal when they have the ball. Although players will usually have many other teammates nearby in front of the goal in a game situation and they must look up to see who is where, they must also learn that their eyes have to be firmly fixed on the ball when shooting it. The most common reason for mis-hit shots is a result of lifting the head as the ball is struck, and consequently not kicking the ball at the intended point. To help encourage players to watch the ball when kicking it, they should be reminded the goal will not move but the ball will, so it is the ball that they must watch when shooting.

©2001 by Prentice Hall

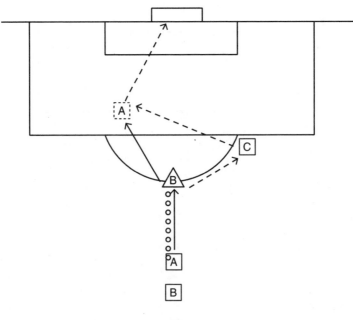

82. DRIBBLE AT SPEED AND SHOOT

Organization:

Line up players one behind the other at about the halfway line facing the goal and the goalkeeper. Each player should have a ball.

Purpose:

To practice shooting a moving ball on goal

Procedure:

Players dribble at full speed and then shoot on goal when they reach the edge of the penalty box. As soon as a player shoots, the next player should begin dribbling so that people are not waiting in line for too long and so the goalkeeper is kept busy.

Coaching points:

Players must practice shooting with both feet, since during a game they will have very little time to control the ball and shoot, and must be able to shoot the ball with either foot depending on how the ball is positioned. Players should shoot low and hard toward the corner of the goal, and follow up their shots in order to take advantage of any rebounded saves that may come back toward them for a second scoring attempt.

NOTE: Although players in the diagram are shown as defender and attacker, all players, regardless of position, should practice this drill.

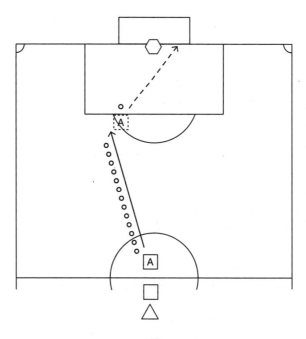

83. MORE DRIBBLING AT SPEED AND SHOOTING

Organization:
Players stand between the penalty box and the halfway line facing the goal and the goalkeeper.

Purpose:
To practice shooting a moving ball on goal

Procedure:
The coach stands behind the players and throws a ball over a player's head and toward the goal, so that as soon as players see the ball in front of them, they must run toward it, dribble it toward the goal, and shoot. The coach will perform this action with each player, one at a time.

Coaching points:
Players must get their shot off as quickly as possible, which may mean shooting a volley or half-volley with the first touch. As players become better at shooting quickly, this drill can be adapted slightly so two players chase and compete for the same ball as it is thrown into play.

©2001 by Prentice Hall

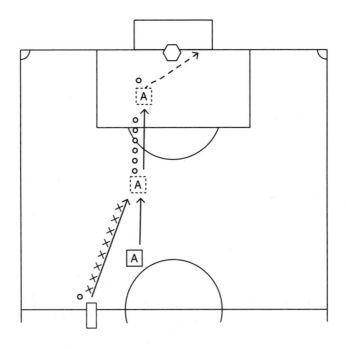

84. TWO PLAYERS SPRINT TO ONE BALL TO SHOOT IT

Organization:

Players form two lines on the goal line facing toward the field and about five yards wide of either goal post. Cones are set up as in the diagram below.

Purpose:

To practice sprinting and shooting

Procedure:

The first player from each line runs around the cone in front of him or her after the coach yells "Go" and races to shoot the ball into the goal.

Coaching points:

Players must be alert and on the balls of their feet so they can be quick off the mark and first to the ball.

Variation:

The drill is set up as above except with players starting in a sitting, kneeling, lying, or other position.

NOTE: Although players in the diagram are shown as holding various positions, all players, regardless of position, should practice this drill.

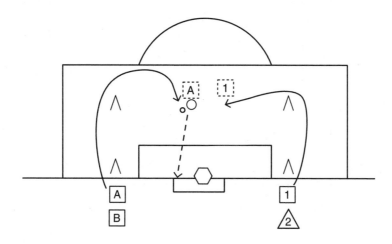

©2001 by Prentice Hall

85. DRIBBLE AND SHOOT

Organization:
Players dribble around cones toward the goal and shoot on goal.

Purpose:
To practice shooting quickly after dribbling toward the goal and reaching a shooting position

Procedure:
Players dribble as fast as they can around the cones and then shoot on goal.

Coaching points:
Players must be able to dribble with their heads up and must remember to watch the ball as they shoot it. Practice dribbling and shooting with both feet.

©2001 by Prentice Hall

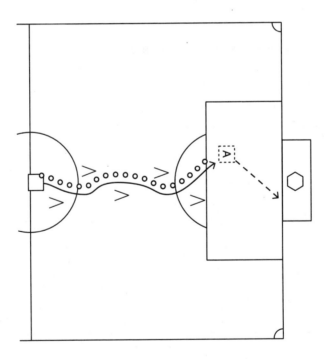

86. DRIBBLE AND SHOOT AT SPEED

Organization:

Players line up at a distance from the goal (20–40 yards).

Purpose:

To practice shooting quickly after dribbling toward the goal and reaching a shooting position

Procedure:

Players dribble as fast as they can toward the goal and shoot the ball before the coach has counted down from five down to one.

Coaching points:

Players must be able to dribble with their heads up and must remember to watch the ball as they shoot it. Players must practice dribbling and shooting with both feet.

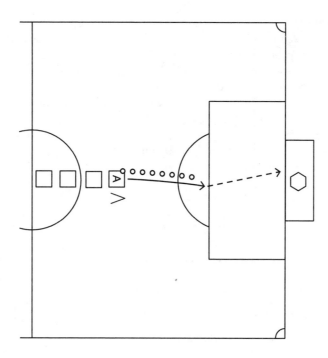

87. PENALTY KICKS

Organization:

Players take turns shooting penalty kicks. Each player uses his or her own ball and waits outside the penalty area while other players are taking their penalty kick.

Purpose:

To practice penalty kicks

Procedure:

A penalty kick is awarded to a team as a result of a direct free kick in the attacking penalty box, and any one player on that team has a free shot on the goalkeeper from the penalty spot. Some players kick the ball as hard as they can with the instep of the foot when taking a penalty shot, while others choose to place the ball more gently and accurately with the inside of the foot. Whichever method is used, it is important that players who will be taking penalty shots during games spend time practicing them during training sessions.

Coaching points:

Players are expected to score goals from penalty shots since they are shooting a stationary ball at the goalkeeper from only a short distance away. Goalkeepers will sometimes make great saves and sometimes lucky saves. Players will also sometimes miss the goal altogether. Obviously there is a certain amount of pressure on players who take penalty kicks, especially when missing the goal could cost their team the game. However, players will miss far less penalties if they practice taking them, have confidence in themselves, try to confuse the goalkeeper by not making it obvious toward which corner the kick will go, and, most important, if they watch the ball as it is kicked and do not look at the intended target.

©2001 by Prentice Hall

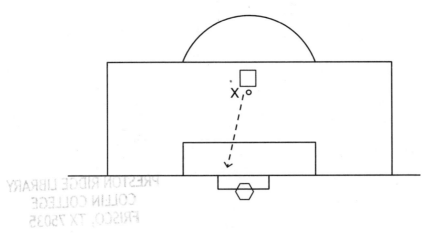

88. DRIBBLING TO GOAL TO SHOOT WITH AN OPPONENT CHALLENGING FOR THE BALL

Organization:

Two players stand side by side about three yards apart on the halfway line, facing the goal and the goalkeeper.

Purpose:

To practice running at speed with the ball and shooting while under pressure

Procedure:

The coach serves a ball by passing it along the ground between the two players toward the goal. As soon as the two players see the ball go past them, they chase after it and compete to win the ball, dribble it to goal, and shoot. The serve can also be chipped or thrown to make it more difficult for the players to control the ball as they compete for it. The drill can also be set up whereby the players sit, lie, or squat on the floor before the ball is kicked into play, so the race for the ball begins by them first rising as quickly as possible from the sitting, lying, or squatting position.

Coaching points:

Players must be alert and in the "ready" position on the balls of their feet so they can move quickly off the mark. Shooting a moving ball while running at top speed takes a lot of practice and concentration. Again, watching the ball as it is shot on goal is essential.

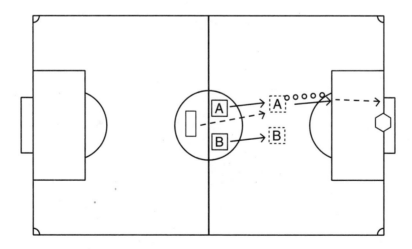

89. LINE SOCCER

Organization:

All players line up side by side on the halfway line facing the goal and the goalkeeper. Each player is given a number.

Purpose:

To practice dribbling, defending, and shooting

Procedure:

The coach calls out two or more numbers as the ball is thrown into play and the players who were called out chase to win the ball and shoot on goal.

Coaching points:

The player who gets to the ball becomes the attacker while the other player becomes the defender. However, if the defender wins the ball, he or she then becomes the attacker. When defending, players must get on the goal side of the ball as quickly as possible, while attackers must use dribbling skills to create enough space and time to take a quick shot at goal.

©2001 by Prentice Hall

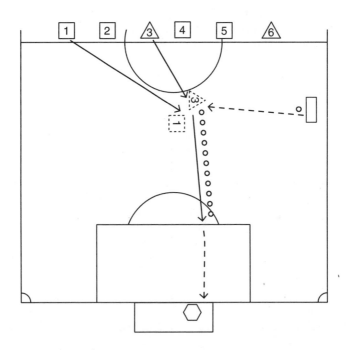

90. THREE PLAYERS DRIBBLE AND PASS THE BALL
TOWARD THE GOAL AND SHOOT

Organization:

Three players stand side by side about three to five yards apart on the halfway line facing the goal and the goalkeeper.

Purpose:

To practice passing the ball into the path of a teammate
To practice shooting a moving ball from the edge of the penalty box

Procedure:

The player in the middle starts with the ball and passes it either to the player on the left or the player on the right. Passers of the ball then follow their pass and run behind and around the outside of the player they passed to, so the receiving player now becomes the player in the middle. The receiver of the ball, meanwhile, moves to meet the ball and passes it to the third player, and then follows the pass and runs around the outside and behind the receiving player. This is done as the players are moving all the time toward the goal, so the player receiving the pass always becomes the middle player and moves to the outside position in the direction the ball is passed.

Coaching points:

Players must judge their runs so they do not find themselves ahead of a pass coming toward them. The shot should be taken when players find they have the ball in their possession and are about at the edge of the penalty box.

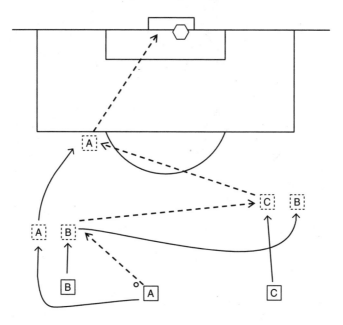

91. ONE PLAYER VERSUS THE GOALKEEPER

Organization:

Players start about 20–30 yards away from the goal with a ball.

Purpose:

To practice scoring with only the goalkeeper to beat

Procedure:

The player approaches the goal and may shoot the ball at any time in order to beat the goalkeeper and score a goal.

Coaching points:

The goalkeeper will move off the goal line to come toward the player with the ball. The player must either decide to attempt to dribble the ball around the goalkeeper to score or to shoot wide of the goalkeeper and into the goal by looking for the largest available open area of the goal at which to shoot.

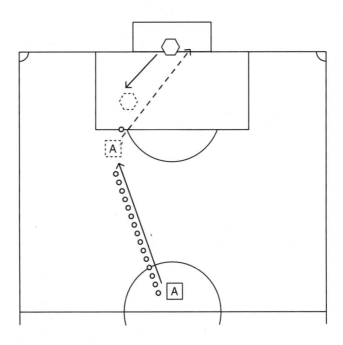

92. VOLLEYING

Organization:
Players line up one behind the other about 10 yards outside the penalty box, facing the goal and goalkeeper.

Purpose:
To get used to volleying the ball

Procedure:
Players take turns passing a ball to a player standing on the edge of the penalty box who either flicks the ball or picks up the ball to serve it to one side for the player to run toward and volley on goal.

Coaching points:
Players must watch the ball very closely when they perform a volley, since taking eyes off the ball for a split second will usually result in the ball being miskicked and going away from the intended target. Instep and inside foot volleys are the most commonly performed volleys, with instep volleys used for power and distance, and inside of the foot volleys used for accuracy and shorter passes or shots. Timing is essential when volleying the ball, so players must judge their run toward the served ball when they will shoot on goal. Players must practice both left and right foot volleys.

Variation:
Players line up and pass the ball toward a server, but now the server plays the return passes along the floor as well as in the air, so players practice shooting a moving ball on the ground as well as in the air. Again, players must practice using both feet for shooting. During a game they may have very little time in which to get a shot off, and if players need time to bring the ball to their preferred foot, they may lose a good goal-scoring opportunity.

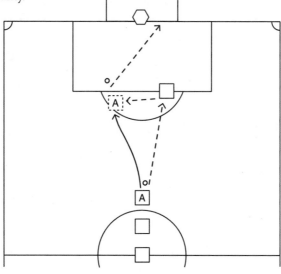

93. SHOOTING THE BALL LOW AND HARD TOWARD THE CORNERS OF THE GOAL

Organization:

Players shoot on an empty goal; both corners/sides of the goal are marked off with cones or corner flags.

Purpose:

To encourage players to shoot low and toward the corners of the goals

Procedure:

Players practice shooting toward the lower corners of the goal, with the area between each cone and goal post the target. This drill can be conducted with players shooting a stationary ball, dribbling the ball to the edge of the penalty box and shooting a moving ball, performing a wall pass and shooting the return pass, or in any other manner the coach decides upon.

Coaching points:

After looking to see where they wish to shoot the ball, players must watch the ball closely. Players must practice shooting at speed and not dwelling on the ball; it is very rare that players will have a lot of time to think when a shooting opportunity arises in a real game.

©2001 by Prentice Hall

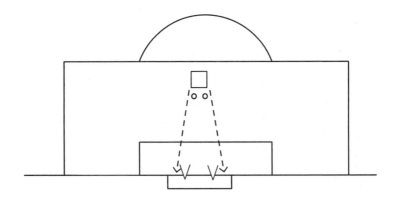

94. SHOOTING THE BALL LOW AND HARD TOWARD THE FAR CORNER

Organization:

Players dribble toward the goal and shoot at the far corner while a teammate from the opposite side of the field follows in on the shot for any rebounds the goalie may direct back into the field of play.

Purpose:

To practice shooting low and hard toward the far corner of the goal
To follow up on shots for possible rebounds

Procedure:

Players dribble toward the goal and take a shot from the edge of the penalty box aiming for the far side corner of the goal, shooting low and hard. A teammate on the other side of the field moves with the player on the ball and takes advantage of any rebounded saves that may come his or her way.

Coaching points:

Shots aimed toward the far post produce more rebounds for other players to follow up on, and usually result in a bigger area of the goal to aim at due to the near-post positioning of the goalkeeper. Players moving in for the rebound must also practice staying onside and must time their runs carefully.

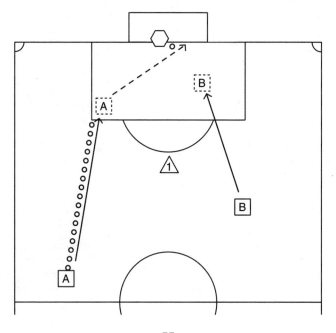

95. DRIBBLE, PASS, CROSS, SHOOT

Organization:

Three players stand side by side about five yards apart on the halfway line facing the goal and the goalkeeper.

Purpose:

To practice passing the ball into the path of a teammate

To practice crossing the ball from the wings so another player may shoot a moving ball from the edge of the penalty box

Procedure:

The player in the middle starts with the ball and passes it either to the player on the left or the player on the right. Passers of the ball then follow their pass and run behind and around the outside of the player they passed to, so the receiving player becomes the player in the middle. The receiver of the ball, meanwhile, moves to meet the ball and passes it to the third player and then follows the pass and runs around the outside and behind the receiving player. This is done as the players are moving toward the goal, so the player receiving the pass always becomes the middle player and moves to the outside position in the direction the ball is passed. When the players get close to the penalty box, a pass is made wide to one of the wings so the player on that side can run wide and cross the ball into the penalty area for the other two players to either head or shoot into the goal. The crosser of the ball should take the ball to the endline before crossing it, and the two players in the penalty box must time their runs so they arrive near the goal as the ball also arrives. One player should run toward the near post for a short cross, and one player should run towards the back post for a long cross.

Coaching points:

Players must judge their runs from the edge of the penalty box as the crossed ball comes over from the wing.

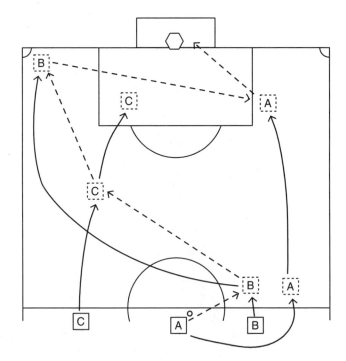

©2001 by Prentice Hall

96. BACK-HEEL, TURN, AND SHOOT

Organization:

Players stand with backs to the goal and a ball at their feet 25 yards from the goal.

Purpose:

To practice turning and shooting quickly

Procedure:

Players take turns at back-heeling the ball, turning, and shooting on goal from about 20 yards.

Coaching points:

Players must perform this drill at speed just as they would have to in a real game. A goalie can also be added to try to save the shots.

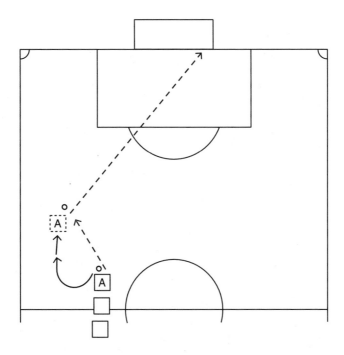

Section 3

TRAPPING

Section 3

TRAPPING

Trapping the ball in soccer refers to stopping or slowing down the ball with any part of the body—other than the hands or arms—in order to bring it under control. Being able to control the ball is one of the most fundamental skills in soccer and is used by all players during every game. Bringing the ball under control does not always necessarily mean bringing it to a complete stop, but more simply means putting the ball in a position that will allow players to do what they want with it next, whether it be a pass, a shot, clearing the ball up the field, or running with the ball. There are three common ways to trap the ball or bring it under control: with the foot, thigh, or chest.

Foot traps

Whatever part of the body is used to trap the ball, it will, in effect, simply be used to try to take the weight off the ball or cushion it so it does not bounce away from the player. To do this, players must draw back the part of the body they are using in the same line and direction the ball is traveling as it arrives. To help achieve this, it is a good idea to have players imagine the ball is an egg or a delicate glass object; this helps them imagine how simply allowing it to hit the foot will cause it to break, whereas drawing the foot away upon arrival will prevent breakage. The aim in trapping the ball is to bring the ball under control with one touch so the second touch can be used to do whatever is desired. Players will find as they start to play in games that they will need to control the ball quickly with one touch since opposing players give them very little time before trying to put in a tackle.

Trapping with the inside of the foot

Trapping the ball with the inside of the foot is the most common way to control a ball coming on the ground toward a player. This is also one of the most effective methods, since the ball can be controlled and positioned for the next move all in the same motion, or even passed off in the same movement.

METHOD

- Move the body so it is in line with the movement of the ball.

- Keep the eyes firmly fixed on the ball.

- Turn the trapping foot out so that it is at 90 degrees to the ball and about six inches off the ground, with the knee slightly bent.

- As the ball arrives, cushion the weight of the ball by drawing the leg and foot back, and at the same time the lower part of the leg must be leaned slightly over the ball to create a wedge between the foot and the ground. The ankle, leg, and foot must remain relaxed.

Trapping with the sole of the foot

Another way of controlling the ball with the foot is with the sole of the foot. However, this method will bring the ball to a standstill and it can take longer to get the ball moving again to produce an effective second touch. This method should not, therefore, be used when players are under pressure and have very little time before they must release the ball.

METHOD

- Move the body so it is in line with the movement of the ball.
- Keep the eyes firmly fixed on the ball, right until it touches the foot.
- As the ball arrives, lift the trapping foot, keeping the knee bent and relaxed.
- As the ball arrives, wedge the ball between the foot and ground, keeping the ankle relaxed.

Thigh traps

The thigh trap is used to trap a ball that is coming toward players in the air, or bouncing toward them. The principles of basic trapping still apply in that players must cushion the weight of the ball with their thigh, and let it drop to their feet as quickly as possible so they may proceed with their next move. The inside, outside, or top of the thigh can be used to bring the ball under control, but the top part of the thigh is the part most commonly used.

METHOD

- Move the body so it is in line with the flight of the ball.

- Judge the flight of the ball, and move accordingly so the ball will arrive at the thigh.

- Lift the thigh so it is horizontal to the ground.

- Allow the ball to hit the middle of the thigh, while at the same time dropping the knee to cushion and take the weight off the ball.

- Allow the ball to drop to the feet, where a foot trap is used to prepare for the next move.

A NOTE ON TRAPPING THE BALL WITH THE THIGH

The inside of the foot, outside of the foot, and the instep can also be used to trap the ball in the air. The same principles apply in that players simply cushion the ball and take the weight off it with their foot, except that they are now doing this while the ball is still in the air. Controlling the ball in the air is difficult but players will find that with practice they will improve dramatically at this skill.

Chest traps

The method of trapping the ball with the upper chest to bring it under control is used for balls that are too high to be trapped with either the feet or the thighs, but are lower than the neck. There are two ways of controlling the ball with the chest, depending upon whether the ball is coming to the player from very high, or traveling to them at chest height parallel to the ground. As with all methods of trapping, the aim is to get the ball under control as quickly as possible, and down to the feet ready for the next move.

Chest control method for a ball approaching at chest height

- Position the body in line with the flight of the ball.

- Extend the arms outward and slightly forward of the body.

- As the ball arrives and hits the chest, withdraw the chest to cushion the ball by bending at the waist and breathing out.

- This will direct the ball down to the feet, ready for the next move.

Chest control method for a high, dropping ball

- Position the body in line with the flight of the ball.

- Extend the arms outward but not forward of the body.

- Lean slightly backward.

- As ball arrives, cushion it by leaning back further.

- The ball will roll down the body and drop to the feet ready for the next move.

TRAPPING DRILLS

97. PASS AND CONTROL

Organization:

Two players stand about 5 to 10 yards apart and pass the ball to each other.

Purpose:

To help players become accustomed to trapping the ball with their feet

Procedure:

Players pass the ball to each other and control it with the inside or the sole of their foot before passing the ball back. Players must practice passing the ball and controlling the ball with both feet and not simply using their preferred foot every time.

Coaching points:

Players must pull back their leg and foot as the ball arrives to take the weight off the pass and cushion the ball as they control it. Players must also keep their eye on the ball as it is controlled. Obviously this drill can be performed using more than two players.

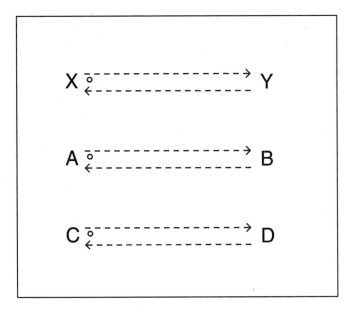

98. TRAPPING THE BALL USING THE FEET

Organization:

One player (without a soccer ball) stands within a circle formed by the other players acting as servers (each with a soccer ball).

Purpose:

To practice trapping the ball with the feet

Procedure:

Servers throw one ball at a time to the receiver in the middle of the circle. The receiver must control the ball and pass it back to the server before receiving a ball from another server. The receiver should use his or her feet to control the ball before passing it back as quickly as possible.

Coaching points:

Receivers should call for the ball each time they receive a serve by calling the server's name.

©2001 by Prentice Hall

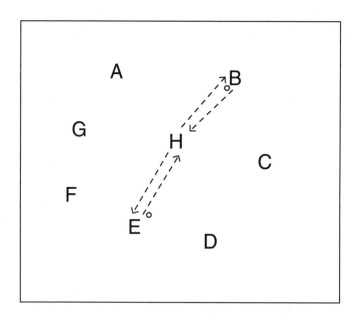

99. PLAYERS PRACTICING BALL CONTROL ON THEIR OWN

Organization:

Each player has a ball and finds a space in which to work.

Purpose:

To practice controlling the ball with feet, thigh, and chest

Procedure:

Players throw the ball in the air and practice using their feet, thigh, and chest to trap the ball. Players should practice moving off quickly over a few yards with the ball (just as they would often do in a game) after controlling the ball.

Coaching points:

Players should ensure that they also practice with their weaker foot. Watching the ball all the way onto the body part to be used for trapping the ball is essential to controlling the ball well.

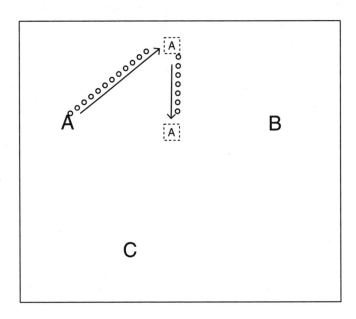

100. TRAPPING THE BALL AND SETTING IT UP FOR THE NEXT PASS ALL IN ONE MOVE

Organization:

Two players stand about 10 yards apart with one ball.

Purpose:

To practice trapping the ball and setting it up for the next pass all in one move

Procedure:

Players pass to each other and control the ball, except now they must concentrate on setting the ball up for the return pass as soon as they receive and control it. Players should do this by controlling the ball and pushing it forward and to one side all in one movement, so the next movement can be the passing of the ball.

Coaching points:

Players must also remember to meet the ball as it comes toward them and not to simply wait for it to arrive. All skills are more effective if practiced as much as possible in the manner they would be carried out in a game; in this drill, this would mean meeting the ball and controlling it and setting it up as quickly as possible for the next pass, just as a player usually has to do in a game when opponents will be challenging or about to be challenging for the ball.

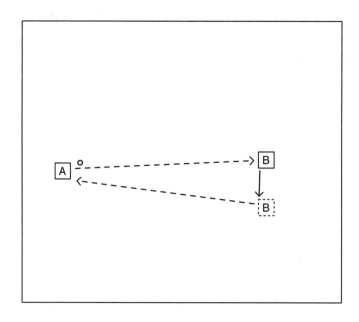

101. CONTROL, PASS, AND MOVE

Organization:

Two lines of players face each other about 10 yards apart.

Purpose:

To practice controlling the ball and then moving away after a pass has been made

Procedure:

The player at the front of line A passes the ball to the player at the front of line B, who controls the ball and passes the ball back to the new player at the front of line A. Meanwhile the initial front player from line A runs to the back of line B, and the initial receiver of the ball in line B runs to the back of line A after passing the ball off.

Coaching points:

Good control is important in this drill, as well as moving to meet the ball, controlling it quickly, passing it back quickly, and then sprinting to the end of the other line. Players should call for the ball when they receive it and call the name of the player they will pass it to next, since calling is a very important but often ignored part of soccer. Players must practice using both feet to trap and pass the ball.

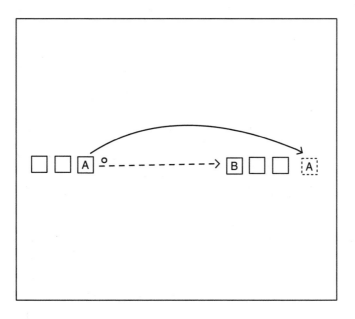

102. DECIDE WHICH PART OF THE BODY TO USE TO CONTROL THE BALL, PASS, AND MOVE

Organization:

Two lines of players face each other about 30 yards apart.

Purpose:

To practice controlling the ball and then moving away after a pass has been made

Procedure:

The player at the front of line A passes a long ball to the player at the front of line B, who must decide whether to use the foot, thigh, chest, or head to control the ball before passing the ball back to the new player at the front of line A. Meanwhile the initial front player from line A runs to the back of line B, and the initial receiver of the ball in line B runs to the back of line A after passing the ball off.

Coaching points:

Players must move to meet the ball, control it quickly, pass it back quickly, and then sprint off quickly just as they would have to in a real game. Players must practice using both feet to trap and pass the ball.

©2001 by Prentice Hall

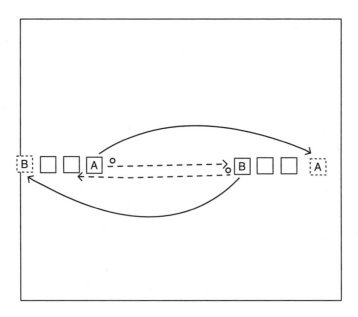

103. TRAPPING PRACTICE WITH THE FEET, THIGH, AND CHEST

Organization:

Two players stand about five yards apart with one ball between them.

Purpose:

To practice trapping with different parts of the body

Procedure:

One player serves the ball at different heights to the receiver, who must decide how to bring the ball under control and pass it back.

Coaching points:

Players receiving and controlling the ball must be alert and on the balls of their feet, so they move toward the ball or adjust their position to judge the flight of the ball for a thigh or chest trap. Players should also be relaxed when controlling the ball, so bodies are not stiff and inflexible (which will cause the ball to bounce away from them when trying to control the ball). When trapping the ball with the chest, care must be taken that the arms do not touch the ball, since this constitutes hand-ball in a game and a free kick will be awarded to the opposing team.

Variation:

The drill is set up as above except after trapping the ball, the player receiving the ball must move off quickly over a few yards while dribbling the ball before passing it back.

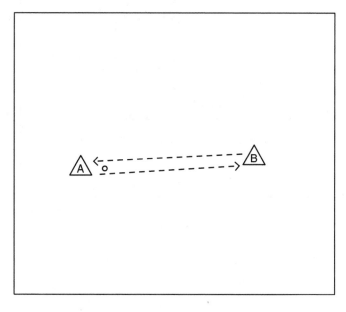

104. TRAP THE BALL, TURN, AND SHOOT

Organization:

Two players stand about five yards apart just outside the penalty box with one ball between them.

Purpose:

To practice trapping the ball and then turning to shoot

Procedure:

One player serves the ball at different heights to the receiver, who must decide how to bring the ball under control and turn to shoot.

Coaching points:

Players receiving and controlling the ball must meet the ball and then turn and shoot as quickly as possible. A defender may be introduced to make the drill more realistic to a real game situation.

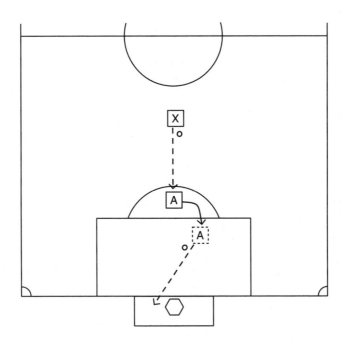

105. CONTROLLING THE BALL UNDER PRESSURE

Organization:

One server, one receiver, and one player marking the receiver very closely from behind stand in a line.

Purpose:

To encourage players to move to the ball to meet and control it quickly

Procedure:

The server passes the ball to the receiver who has a defender marking him or her very closely from behind. The receiver must move to the ball and bring it under control before passing it back to the server. The defender should simply put pressure on the receiver as the drill is first introduced, but should actually challenge for the ball as the practice develops and the receiver improves his/her ball control.

Coaching points:

A receiver must be quick off the mark to control the ball before the defender challenges and tackles for the ball.

Variation:

As players become better at controlling the ball, the servers should pass the ball at different heights and speeds so the receiver must decide whether to use the feet, thigh, or chest to control the ball.

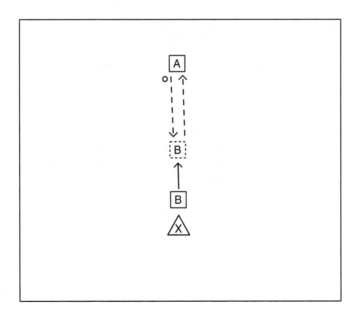

106. TRAPPING THE BALL USING THE FEET, THIGH, CHEST, AND HEAD

Organization:

One player (without a soccer ball) stands inside a circle of other players acting as servers.

Purpose:

To practice trapping the ball using different parts of the body

Procedure:

Each server throws a ball to the receiver in the middle of the circle, who must control the ball and pass it back to the server before receiving a ball from another server. The receiver should use the feet, thigh, or chest to control the ball before passing it back as quickly as possible.

Coaching points:

It is very important for receivers to call for the ball each time they receive a serve by calling the server's name.

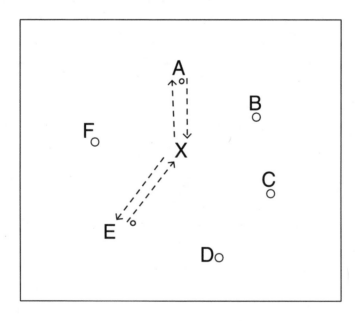

107. TRAP THE BALL AND PASS IT OFF
TO ANOTHER PLAYER

Organization:

Four players stand inside a circle with all other players acting as servers (half with soccer balls).

Purpose:

To trap the ball while using vision to plan who the controlled ball will go to next

Procedure:

Servers throw their ball to a receiver in the middle of the circle, who must control the ball and pass it back to another server without a ball before receiving a ball from another server. The receiver should use the feet, thigh, or chest to control the ball before passing it back as quickly as possible.

Coaching points:

Players should head the ball directly back to the server if the ball is arriving higher than chest high, and they do not have time or room to step back in order to judge the flight of the ball so it will arrive chest high. Receivers should call for the ball each time they receive a serve by calling the server's name.

NOTE: Although players in the diagram are shown as holding various positions, all players, regardless of position, should practice this drill.

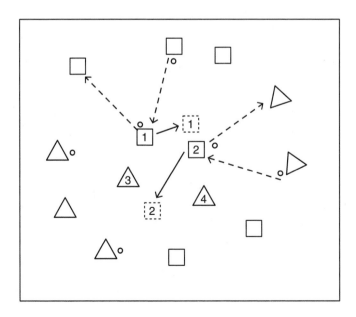

108. MOVING TOWARD THE BALL WHEN TRAPPING IT, AND THEN PASSING IT OFF QUICKLY

Organization:

Three players: Two servers stand about 10 yards apart (each with a ball) with one receiver between them.

Purpose:

To meet the ball, bring it under control, and pass it off as quickly as possible

Procedure:

The receiver runs toward one server and controls a pass coming toward him or her and then passes the ball back. The receiver then turns and moves toward the other server who passes to him or her in the same way so the ball can again be controlled and passed back.

Coaching points:

Players must move to meet the ball and keep their eyes on the ball until it is under control.

Variation:

The drill is set up as above, except the servers throw the ball to the receiver's thigh or chest. The receiver must control the ball with either the thigh or chest and pass the ball back the first time as it drops toward the feet before it hits the ground.

©2001 by Prentice Hall

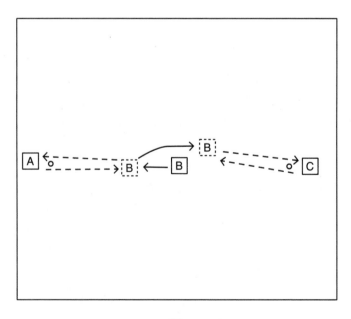

109. CONTROLLING THE BALL WITH A VOLLEY

Organization:
Three players: Two servers stand about 10 yards apart (each with a ball) with one receiver between them.

Purpose:
To meet the ball and pass it back to the server with a volley

Procedure:
The receiver runs toward one server and volleys the ball back. The receiver then turns and moves toward the other server who passes it in the same way so the ball can again be volleyed back.

Coaching points:
Players must move to meet the ball, and keep their eyes on the ball while volleying it.

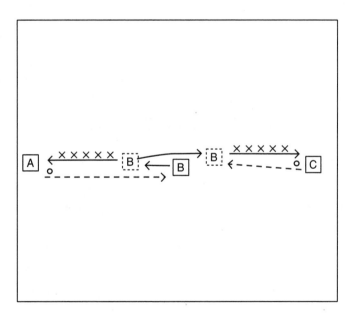

Section 4

DRIBBLING

Section 4

DRIBBLING

When players have the ball under control, they must be able to run and kick the ball along the ground at the same time, commonly known in soccer as dribbling with the ball. Players must be able to dribble with the inside and outside of both feet and must be able to change speed and direction, all while either simply moving the ball along unchallenged or, more difficultly, while trying to get around an opposing player. Although attackers and midfielders will use dribbling skills the most when trying to go around opposing players to score goals or create goal-scoring opportunities, defenders are also required to dribble past players at times when they have no passing or clearing option available or when they have pushed forward to help the offense.

Dribbling is one more of the fundamental elements of soccer and can never be practiced enough no matter what the skill level of the player. Players must learn to keep the ball near them under close control and feel totally relaxed and comfortable when moving with the ball. They must also learn to not look at the ball all the time while dribbling, but must be able to look up to see where opposing players and teammates are positioned.

The basics of dribbling

- Players must not let the ball get too far ahead of them. Taking short strides will help to achieve this (except when running as quickly as possible).

- Players must keep their heads up as much as possible to see teammates and opposing team members.

- Players must be able to use both feet.

- Players kick the ball gently with either the inside or outside of the foot. They must not use the toes to kick the ball but must use the inside or outside part of the foot closest to the toes.

- When running fast with the ball, most players use the outside of the foot to move the ball along since this fits in more naturally with the players' longer strides. (Having said this, it is okay to use the inside, outside, or both; whichever method feels the most comfortable for a player is best.)

Shielding the ball

When players are dribbling the ball while being marked, they must shield the ball. This means making sure their body is between the ball and the opposing team member, so as to make it more difficult for the ball to be tackled away from them. As defenders move closer to the ball, attackers must change position to continue shielding the ball by controlling the ball using the leg farther from the opponent. Obviously being able to kick well with both feet will greatly help when shielding the ball.

DRIBBLING DRILLS

110. MOVING AROUND IN ANY SPACE OR PART OF THE FIELD WHILE DRIBBLING THE BALL

Organization:

Each player has a ball and finds plenty of space.

Purpose:

To help players feel comfortable when dribbling with the ball

Procedure:

Players simply run around with the ball in order to get used to having the ball at their feet. They must look at the ball as little as possible, but instead must get used to playing with their heads up so they can see teammates, opponents, and space. Players should also practice changing the pace of their dribbling from a normal jogging speed to a quick 5- or 10-yard sprint with the ball.

Coaching points:

Coaches must watch to check that players keep their heads up and focused on what is going on around them, and do not simply look down at the ball all the time. Players must practice dribbling so they can feel where the ball is and do not have to look at it all the time.

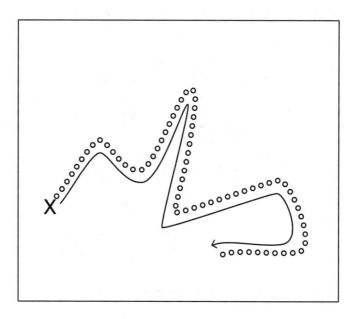

111. KEEPING THE HEAD UP WHILE DRIBBLING INSIDE A GRID

Organization:

Players are inside a grid or circle, each with his or her own ball.

Purpose:

To teach players to dribble with their heads up since they must see where other players are in order to avoid them

Procedure:

Players must dribble around with their own ball and without bumping into other players.

Coaching points:

Players should be encouraged to use all the space within the grid, so they are constantly looking for and moving to a new space. If someone else heads to the space where they were heading, they simply look for another free space, all the time while moving with the ball. As players improve at this drill, they should dribble around quicker, even with a 5- or 10-yard sprint carried out at the blow of the whistle, or a change of direction at the blow of two whistles. Obviously the number of players and size of the grid can make this drill more or less difficult.

©2001 by Prentice Hall

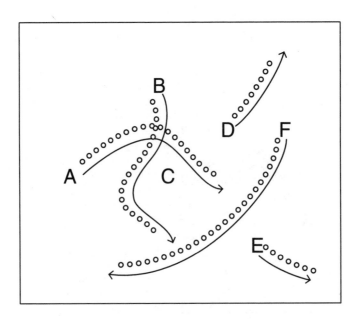

112. KNOCKOUT

Organization:
Players are inside a grid or circle, each with his or her own ball.

Purpose:
To teach players to dribble with their heads up since they must see where other players are in order to avoid being tackled

Procedure:
Players must dribble around with their own ball while at the same time trying to kick other balls out of the grid. The last player left in is the winner.

Coaching points:
Players must shield their own ball and keep their heads up to see where other players are in all directions.

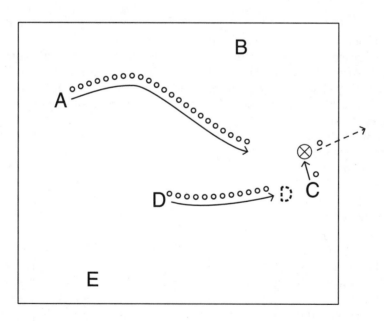

113. RUNNING ACROSS THE FIELD WHILE DRIBBLING WITH THE BALL

Organization:

Players stand side-by-side along the touch-line, about two to three yards apart, and dribble with their own ball across the field.

Purpose:

To practice dribbling with the ball at different speeds

Procedure:

Players all dribble together across the field at the same pace, while keeping the distance between themselves and other players the same. Players practice dribbling with the inside of their foot only, then the outside of their foot only, then alternating one touch with the inside followed by one touch with the outside of the foot. When players dribble fast with the ball, they will usually find they naturally dribble with the outside of the foot, while when dribbling slower they will use both the inside and the outside. Players should, therefore, be encouraged to practice and try with both the inside and the outside so they can determine which feels more comfortable and effective for them. This is also a good drill to use to force players to use and practice with their weaker kicking foot. This is achieved by players dribbling solely with their left foot for some time and then solely with their right foot.

The coach should also instruct players to change the speed of dribbling during this drill. At the blow of a whistle, players should sprint with the ball over 5 or 10 yards and then slow down again. A change of pace is very important in soccer, especially for attackers who can leave the defenders who are marking them behind by switching from dribbling slowly with the ball one second to sprinting with the ball the next.

Coaching points:

Coaches must ensure players dribble the ball with their heads up, that they do not kick the ball with their toes, and that they keep the ball under control at close quarters rather than kicking it a few yards in front and then chasing after it.

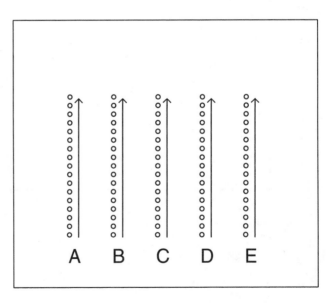

©2001 by Prentice Hall

114. DRIBBLING AROUND CONES

Organization:

Place five cones in a line about two to three yards apart for players to dribble around.

Purpose:

To help players change direction when dribbling whether it be to beat an opponent or to run with the ball into space (Although cones cannot tackle players, they act as an excellent means of encouraging players to change directions while dribbling.)

Procedure:

Players form a line at the first cone and take turns dribbling in and out of the cones to the end and then back again. Players should practice using both feet to dribble.

Coaching points:

Players must look up while dribbling and must keep the ball under close control by not allowing it to travel too far in front of them.

NOTE: It is quite often a good idea to have two or three sets of cones set up next to each other for this drill and for drills 115 through 121 so the players can be split into groups that race against each other. This not only encourages players to perform the drill faster since they are racing, but it also ensures that players have more turns at each exercise and do not wait around in line longer than necessary. However, coaches must watch that players perform the drill correctly when racing and do not simply replace correct technique with speed.

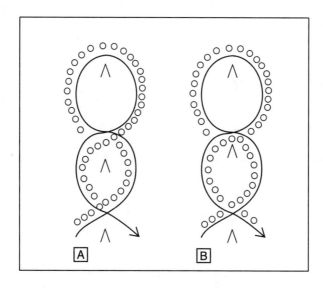

115. CIRCLES AND SQUARES

Organization:

Set cones in a circle or square formation.

Purpose:

To help players keep their heads up as much as possible when dribbling

Procedure:

Players form a line at the first cone. The first player dribbles around the cones in a clockwise direction. When the first player has reached the second cone, the second player begins, and so on. This ensures that players are practicing at the same time rather than waiting in line for too long.

Coaching points:

Players must look up as much as possible while dribbling.

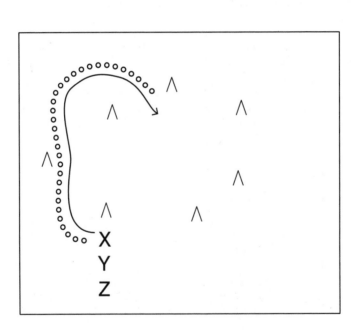

116. SPRINT

Organization:

Place two cones about ten yards apart.

Purpose:

To help players dribble at speed—an essential skill during a game

Procedure:

Players form a line at the first cone. Players take turns dribbling as fast as they can to the second cone, turning around by dragging the ball back with the sole of the foot and dribbling back to the first cone. Players should practice using both feet to dribble.

Coaching points:

Players must be able to dribble at full speed and still keep the ball under control and away from any opponents trying to tackle them.

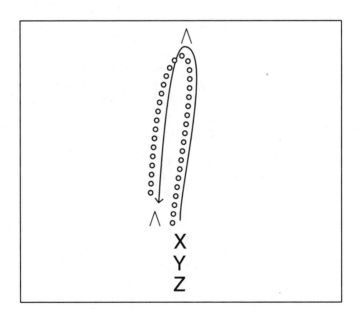

117. AROUND THE CONE

Organization:

Set up two cones about ten yards apart.

Purpose:

To help players practice dribbling and keeping the ball very close to them

Procedure:

Players form a line at the first cone. They take turns dribbling to the second cone where they dribble the ball in a complete circle around the cone before dribbling back.

Coaching points:

Encourage players to perform this drill at speed to make it realistic to the game situation. This can be achieved by having two or more lines of players racing against each other at other cones.

©2001 by Prentice Hall

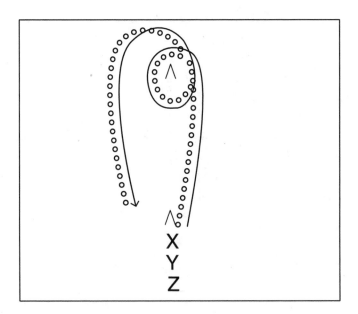

118. FIRST AND BACK

Organization:

Place four cones in a line about five yards apart.

Purpose:

To provide dribbling practice and fitness exercise at the same time

Procedure:

Players form a line at the first cone and take turns dribbling to the second cone, then back to the first cone; to the third cone, then back to the first, and so on until they have reached all cones. Players should practice using both feet to dribble.

Coaching points:

Players must look up while dribbling and must dribble as fast as possible between the cones and make well-controlled turns at the cones. Encourage players to practice different methods of turning at each cone.

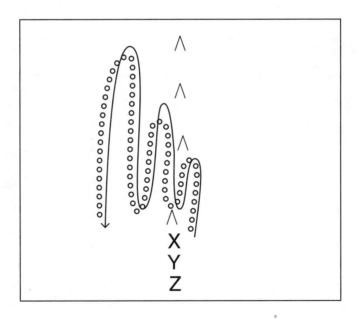

119. DRIBBLE AND PASS

Organization:

Set up two cones 15 yards apart.

Purpose:

To practice speed dribbling and accuracy passing

Procedure:

Players form a line at the first cone. The first player dribbles as quickly as possible to the second cone and then passes the ball back to the next player. The first player remains at the second cone until all other players end up at the second cone.

Coaching points:

The pass back to the next player in line should be an accurate firm pass. The player receiving the ball should come to meet the ball.

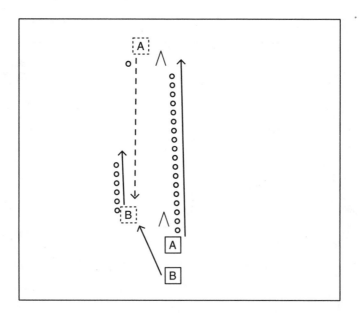

120. WEAK FOOT

Organization:

Place five cones in a line about two to three yards apart for players to dribble around.

Purpose:

To practice dribbling and passing with the weaker foot

Procedure:

Players form a line at the first cone and take turns dribbling in and out of the cones to the end, where they stop and pass the ball back to the next player in line. Players may use only their weaker foot to dribble and pass the ball.

Coaching points:

The only way to improve the weaker foot is through practice. Although drills such as this where only the weaker foot can be used may seem unrealistic, they serve as excellent practice.

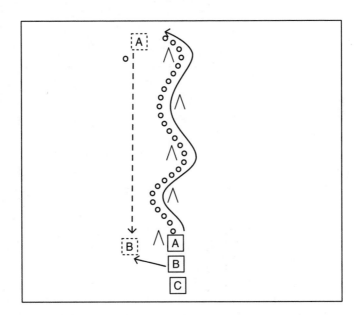

121. LEAVE AND RETRIEVE

Organization:

Place five cones in a line about two to three yards apart. Place four soccer balls at the first cone.

Purpose:

To improve speed dribbling and sprinting

Procedure:

Players form a line at the first cone. The first player dribbles one ball to the second cone, leaves it there, sprints back to the beginning, dribbles another ball to the third cone, sprints back, and so on. The next player sprints to the second cone, dribbles the ball back to the first cone, sprints to the third cone, dribbles the ball back, and so on until all the balls are back at the first cone. The next player then dribbles the ball to the cones just as the first player did.

Coaching points:

Players must dribble at speed with the ball and sprint when they are running back to get the next ball.

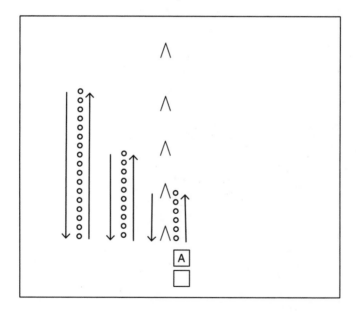

122. DRIBBLING WITH THE HEAD UP

Organization:

Players all stand side by side about five yards apart, each with a ball, and face the coach.

Purpose:

To help players feel the ball at their feet and avoid the necessity to keep looking down

Procedure:

Coaches point in the direction in which the players must dribble with the ball. This could be forward, backward, left, or right. It is important the coach uses hand signals and not vocal commands for the direction changes, so the players must always look up at the coach and not down at their soccer balls.

Coaching points:

Players should look and feel relaxed and comfortable when dribbling a soccer ball. Their eyes must be used as much as possible to see other players in the game, and as little as possible to look at the ball when it is at their feet, except when they first receive and control the ball and when they shoot or pass it and when they occasionally glance down at it while dribbling.

©2001 by Prentice Hall

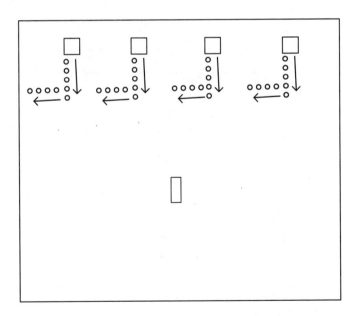

123. DRIBBLING AT SPEED

Organization:

Players line up side by side about three yards apart along one of the sidelines.

Purpose:

To teach players how to dribble while running fast

Procedure:

Players race from one side of the field to the other while dribbling the ball at their feet.

Coaching points:

Players often find they are running toward the goal with only the goalie to beat. However, they must also be able to run fast with the ball against a defender. Coaches must ensure that players do not simply kick the ball way out in front of them and then chase it, but rather keep the ball close enough so the defender will not be able to easily win it.

©2001 by Prentice Hall

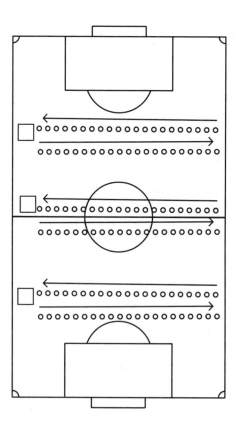

124. DRIBBLE AND PASS

Organization:

Players form two lines, 10 to 15 yards apart, facing each other. Only one ball is needed.

Purpose:

To help players get used to dribbling and passing at the same time

Procedure:

The player with the ball dribbles toward the other line, and about halfway passes the ball to the front person in the other line and continues jogging to the back of the other line. Meanwhile the front player of the other line receives the ball and dribbles halfway toward the facing line before passing the ball in the same manner as the previous player.

Coaching points:

Players receiving the pass must come to meet the ball rather than waiting for the ball to arrive, and should be alert and ready for a bad pass that may not come directly to them.

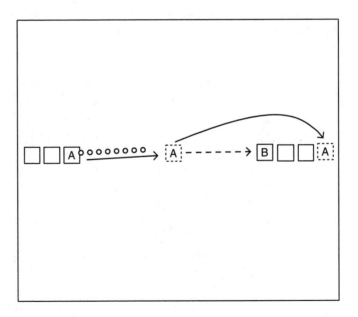

125. DRIBBLE FOUR BALLS TO YOUR BASE

Organization:
Four players stand beside a cone of their own and six balls are set up in the middle.

Purpose:
To practice speed dribbling and the use of good vision

Procedure:
Each player starts at his or her own cone. When the coach blows the whistle, they run to the balls in the middle and may dribble one ball at a time back to their cone. When there are no balls left in the middle, they may dribble balls from other players' cones back to their own. There is no tackling or defending balls. The first player to have four balls at his or her cone is the winner.

Coaching points:
Players need to dribble at speed and must plan where they are going next while they are dribbling the ball. This requires keeping the head up while dribbling.

NOTE: Although players in the diagram are shown as holding various positions, all players, regardless of position, should practice this drill.

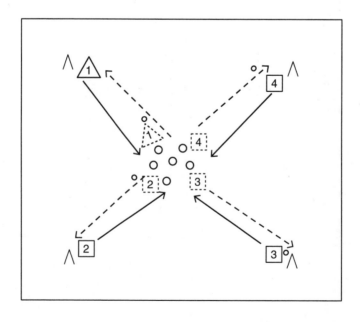

126. FAKES AND DUMMIES

Organization:

One versus one.

Purpose:

To practice taking players on

Procedure:

One player runs at the other with the ball and attempts to get around the other by using a fake. At the beginning of the drill, the defender should not tackle but simply jockey and pressure the player with the ball. However, once the attacker improves at performing fakes and dribbling with the ball, the defender should actually attempt to win the ball.

Coaching points:

Attacking players must not attempt to pass the defender until they are sure they have forced the defender to commit one way as a result of a fake. Players must be able to throw fakes and take off and dribble with either foot in either direction.

Variation:

A goal and goalkeeper are added so that the attacker must now attempt to beat the defender and then shoot on goal.

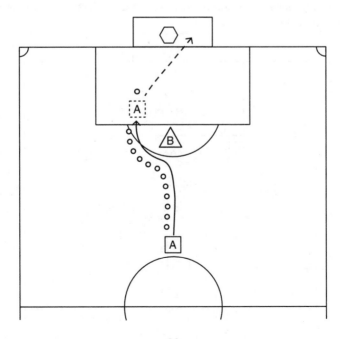

127. DRIBBLING AND THINKING ABOUT
THE NEXT MOVE AT THE SAME TIME

Organization:

Four players: one player with the ball, two teammates, and one defender.

Purpose:

To practice passing while dribbling

Procedure:

Player A with the ball dribbles toward the defender. Upon reaching the defender, player A can pass it to either the teammate on the right or on the left. The attacker then passes the defender and receives a pass back. This is known as a wall pass and is a very simple but effective move. Once players are accustomed to the drill, the defender should attempt to win the ball, and a second defender can be added. In this case, attackers can either pass the ball to their free teammate or beat the defender on their own, depending on whether or not the free teammate is in a good position to receive a pass.

Coaching points:

The player dribbling the ball must keep the head up to determine who to pass to, or whether to beat the defender. When passing the ball, the player who is dribbling must then make a well-timed run into a space to receive a return pass.

Variation:

A goal and goalkeeper are now added, so once the defenders have been beaten, a shot on goal must be taken.

©2001 by Prentice Hall

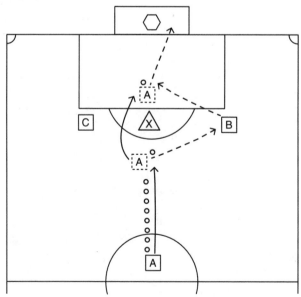

128. DRIBBLE AND RELEASE THE BALL

Organization:
Players form two lines 10 to 15 yards apart and face each other. Only one ball is needed.

Purpose:
To help players get used to dribbling and allow a teammate to take over the ball

Procedure:
The player with the ball dribbles toward the other line, and at about three-fourths the way toward it, the front player takes the ball over and continues dribbling. Player A continues running to back of line B.

Coaching points:
This obviously requires good understanding and communication between the two players so they know exactly when one player will leave the ball and the other will move off with it.

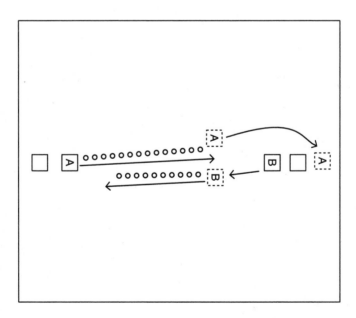

Section 5
TACKLING

Section 5
TACKLING

Tackling in soccer is the term given to the method players use with their feet to try to take the ball away from an opposing player. Tackling is one of the more physical aspects of soccer since although pushing or grabbing the other player is not allowed, leaning with the shoulder is legal. Often misjudged, or indeed well judged tackles, result in players kicking each other in the shins and ankles by mistake (hence, the importance of shinguards).

Tackling is primarily thought of as a move carried out by defenders, but all players, including goalkeepers, must know how to tackle. However, it is the defenders who must be the most proficient at this skill, since they are usually the last player before the goaltender and if they allow an opposing player to get past them, the opposing player will then have a good goal-scoring opportunity. Tackling can involve defenders dispossessing their opponent and winning the ball for themselves, just getting the ball away from the opponent so it goes out of bounds for a throw-in, clearing the ball to a teammate, or creating a loose ball for a defender or someone else to chase down. The most difficult thing about tackling is not the actual challenge for the ball itself, but timing the challenge and deciding exactly when to try to kick/win the ball.

The actual tackle

- Defenders should jockey/maneuver the opponent to one side.

- Defenders must stand on the balls of their feet, with knees bent, ready to move with the attacker.

- Defenders must keep their eyes firmly fixed on the ball rather than on the opposing player.

- Defenders must keep close enough to their opponent so when they do challenge for the ball, they will be able to reach it.

- Defenders must win the ball either by blocking the ball between the inside of their foot and the attacker's foot with all their body weight behind the foot for power, or by kicking the ball out of play or up the field away from danger.

The front-on 50–50 tackle/block tackle

A 50–50 ball refers to a loose ball that two players challenge for with equal chance of gaining possession. In this situation, players will often need to perform a front-on block tackle. Players will meet their opponent front-on and challenge for the ball with the inside of one of their feet, with this foot positioned as though performing a pass with the inside of the foot. They should put all their weight into the tackle, with the ankle locked tight. It is important that they keep their eyes on the ball, so that after the initial block they can see where the ball goes and get their foot to it as quickly as possible. Obviously, tackling is all about determination and players must perform strong challenges with all their weight behind the inside of their foot; they must have no fear, just sheer desire and determination to win the ball.

The slide tackle

There will be times when attackers have either beaten defenders or had a head start on them, and so defenders will need to perform a slide tackle. Timing is probably even more important here, since defenders are the last line of defense before the goalkeeper and a missed tackle not only will provide attackers with a scoring opportunity, but it will also give them plenty of time to try to score while the defender is still getting up from the ground. It is for this reason that slide tackles, although potentially quite effective, should only be used when absolutely necessary.

Slide tackles may only be performed from the front or side, since any tackle from behind will result in a foul being called by the referee. The slide tackle is performed by sliding down to the ground on one leg while at the same time swinging the other leg around to contact with the ball and knock it away from the player to a less dangerous area. It is important not to trip the attacking player and to not perform a block tackle that could result in the ball bouncing off the attacker's legs and remaining in the attacker's path to the goal. (Although defenders usually concentrate on knocking the ball either out of play or to a teammate or a less dangerous position, when slide tackles are performed in the less dangerous midfield and attacking third of the field, tacklers can try to win possession for themselves by blocking the ball and putting it in a position where they can quickly get up and move off with the ball.)

Tackling

It should be noted at this point that although tackling is a very important part of the game, and players must be able to win tackles to gain possession of the ball for their team, it is also very important that players do not injure their teammates during tackling drills. Tackling is the time in soccer when most physical contact occurs, and players should be encouraged to save their aggression and fighting determination for the real games. Coaches often insist that players perform no slide tackles during practice, since this form of tackling can often lead to injuries. Above all, players must remember to wear their shinguards during all practice sessions as well as during games.

TACKLING DRILLS

129. TACKLING AND DRIBBLING

Organization:

All players stand inside a grid or circle, each with a soccer ball except for two players without a ball.

Purpose:

To practice tackling and dribbling

To get players used to playing soccer with their heads up to see what is happening around them

Procedure:

Players who have a ball dribble around inside while players without a ball must tackle and dispossess another player in order to get a ball. Players who lose their balls must tackle a different player in order to get another soccer ball for themselves.

Coaching points:

Vision, effective use of space, tackling, and dribbling are all practiced in this drill.

©2001 by Prentice Hall

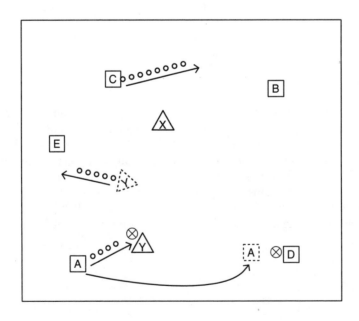

130. ONE VERSUS ONE AGAINST THE GOALKEEPER

Organization:

Players line up one behind the other and take turns running at a defender who is on the edge of the penalty box and who they must beat before shooting on goal.

Purpose:

To practice defending against attackers who have only to beat them before shooting on goal

Procedure:

Defenders should move toward attackers as they approach in order to close them down as soon as possible. They should try to force attackers in the direction of their weaker foot if they know which foot this is, and then wait until the attacker commits before attempting to tackle in the hope that this will distract the attacker and force the shot off target.

Coaching points:

Defenders must watch the ball very closely and not be fooled by the many fakes the attackers will perform in order to beat them. It is good practice for the defenders to have the most skillful and fastest attackers play against them in practice so they are prepared for high-quality attackers in a real game.

©2001 by Prentice Hall

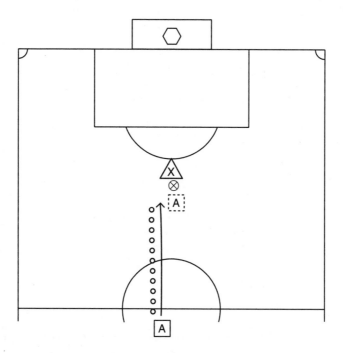

131. DEFENDER CHASES AFTER A BREAKAWAY ATTACKER FROM THE HALFWAY LINE

Organization:
One defender and one attacker are on the halfway line, with a goalie in the goal. The coach throws the ball into play.

Purpose:
To teach defenders to recover goal-side of the ball as quickly as possible when an opponent has a head start on them

Procedure:
The attacker stands on the halfway line facing the goal, and the defender stands two to three yards behind the attacker with back to the attacker. The coach throws the ball toward the goal and shouts "go," so both players race to the ball. The attacker must attempt to score a goal while the defender must get goal side of the ball and try to prevent a goal by tackling the ball away from the attacker and clearing it up field or out for a throw-in or corner kick.

Coaching points:
The defender's first concern is to recover goal-side of the ball and the attacker (which means being between the attacker and the goal), and then to challenge or jockey for the ball as quickly as possible. (If this drill becomes too easy for either the defender or attacker, the distance between them at the start can be adjusted to make the drill more suitable.)

©2001 by Prentice Hall

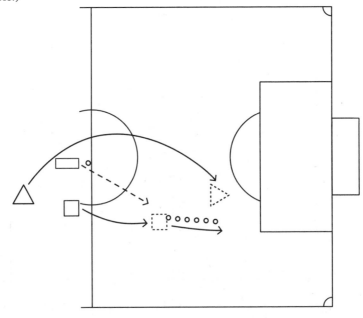

132. JOCKEYING AND CLOSE MARKING

Organization:
One attacking player and one defending player stand in a circle formed by the rest of the players.

Purpose:
To ensure defenders are always ready and alert and can move quickly with the attacker

Procedure:
Half the players standing around the attacker and the defender have soccer balls at their feet and half do not. The attacking player calls to any one of the players with a soccer ball, receives a pass, controls the ball, and passes it back to another player without a soccer ball. The attacker then moves to receive another pass from a different player with a soccer ball and again passes it on to a player without a ball. The defender must move with the attacker and mark very closely so as to hopefully attempt to tackle the attacker. Attackers will obviously try to keep the defender behind at all times, so it is up to defenders to either read a coming pass to intercept it, or mark the attacker very tightly so the attacker cannot turn without being tackled, and must, therefore, look for a pass in front only.

Coaching points:
Defenders must always be in the ready position on the balls of their feet, so they can move with the attacker and hopefully sometimes beat the attacker to a pass.

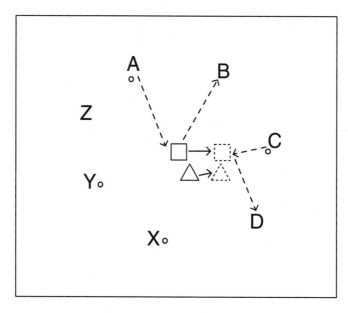

133. FORCING THE ATTACKER TO PLAY THE BALL BACK TOWARD THE TEAM'S OWN HALF

Organization:

One server, one attacker, one defender, one goal with a goalkeeper.

Purpose:

To encourage defenders to mark closely and tightly behind attackers in order to prevent them from turning

Procedure:

Attackers stand with their back to the defenders and the goal, but facing the server who is in front of them. As the attackers receive the ball, they must attempt to turn and face the defender and the goal, so that they can beat the defender and shoot on goal. It is the job of the defenders to mark the attackers very closely so that they can tackle them immediately as they turn, resulting in no shot on goal or prevent them turning and force a pass back to the server.

Coaching points:

Players must properly understand what marking tightly and closely entails: Defenders should stand about an arm's length away from the player they are marking and should be on the balls of their feet ready to move quickly. They must be well balanced, watching the ball at all times and not the player who will be throwing fakes in the hope that defenders will commit themselves in one direction so he or she can move off with the ball in the other direction. When the defender does perform the actual tackle, it must be well timed and accurate.

©2001 by Prentice Hall

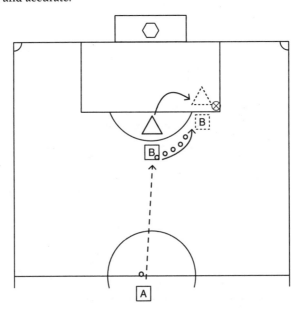

134. TWO VERSUS ONE

Organization:

One server, one attacker, one defender, one goal with a goalkeeper.

Purpose:

To encourage defenders to mark closely and tightly behind attackers in order to prevent them from turning

Procedure:

An attacker stands with back to the defenders and the goal but facing the server who stands in front. On receiving the ball, the attacker must attempt to turn and face the defender and the goal, to beat the defender, and shoot on goal. It is the job of the defenders to mark the attacker very closely so they can tackle him or her immediately as he or she turns, resulting in no shot on goal. The attacker can now pass back to the server and move to receive another pass after moving away to find some more space in which to receive the pass and hopefully turn with the ball.

Coaching points:

This situation makes it more difficult for the defender who is now in effect playing two-on-one. It now becomes even more important that the defender move with the attacker and also keep an eye on the ball which will be passed to the attacker. It is also important that defenders understand that forcing the attacker to play the ball back toward his or her own half is more effective than trying to perform a badly timed tackle that fails and allows the attacker to go past them.

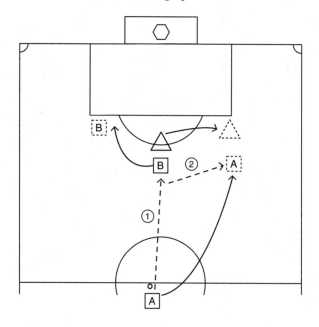

135. JOCKEYING

Organization:

One-on-one in a grid.

Purpose:

To teach players how to jockey their opponent and slow him or her down until defensive help arrives

Procedure:

When players are one-on-one with an opponent and no other players on their team are nearby, they often need to jockey their opponent to slow them down until help arrives or until they absolutely have no choice but to put in a challenge. One player tries to dribble the ball from one side of the grid to the other, while the defender's aim is to slow down this player as much as possible to prevent him or her from getting there, and to only challenge for the ball with a tackle when absolutely certain of winning the ball, or when absolutely necessary.

Coaching points:

Defenders must be well balanced and on the balls of their feet ready to move with the attacker. They should also jockey the attacker to one side by facing them slightly side-on and forcing them to that side.

136. BEAT AN OPPONENT BEFORE PASSING

Organization:

A regular small-sided game or scrimmage.

Purpose:

To create a drill in which plenty of tackling occurs

Procedure:

A regular game is played except that any player who has the ball must attempt to dribble past at least one opponent before passing the ball. If players lose the ball, they may not win the ball directly back by tackling the player who tackled them, but must allow the player who won the ball to move on. This is to ensure that players do not become too clustered together during the drill.

Coaching points:

Obviously this drill is not too realistic in that players are usually encouraged to pass the ball whenever a teammate is in a better position and is unmarked. However, this drill will encourage plenty of tackling practice.

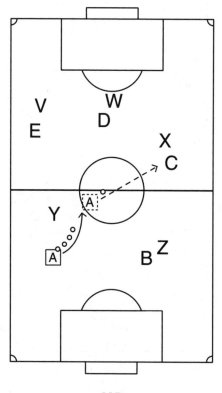

137. KICK OUT

Organization:

All players are inside a grid with their own ball.

Purpose:

To practice tackling, shielding the ball, and dribbling

Procedure:

All players dribble around while attempting to kick other players' balls out of the grid and protect their own ball. A player must sit out when his or her ball is kicked out. The last player left is the winner.

Coaching points:

Shielding the ball is an important part of this drill as well as using good vision and keeping the head up as much as possible.

NOTE: Although players in the diagram are shown as defender and attacker, all players, regardless of position, should practice this drill.

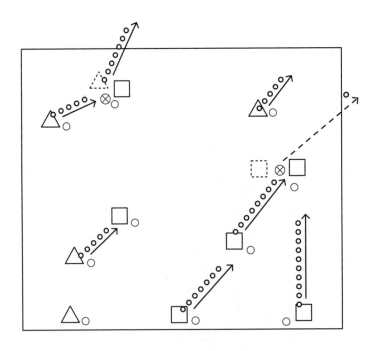

Section 6

THROW-INS

Section 6
THROW-INS

The throw-in is the only time players other than the goalkeeper can use their hands in the game of soccer. A throw-in is called by the referee when the ball travels out of play over one of the sidelines. The ball is awarded to the team that did not touch it last before it left the playing field. There are several specific rules involved in throwing the ball back into play and if these rules are infringed in any way, the ball is awarded to the other team in the form of a throw-in.

Method of throwing the ball in

- The player performing the throw-in must face the playing field.
- Both feet must remain on the ground at the time the ball is actually released and the feet must also be on or behind the sideline.
- Both hands must be used to throw the ball in.
- The hands must start from behind the player's head and must pass over the head before the ball is released.
- The throw-in must be performed in one continuous motion.

Throw-ins, although fairly simple to perform once a player learns how, are a very important part of the game. One of the fundamental elements of success for a soccer team is winning and keeping possession of the ball. A throw-in, therefore, should be practiced and mastered so throwers can throw the ball accurately wherever they want it to go, whether it be to a teammate's foot or into a space for them to run to. Throw-ins that are taken quickly are very effective since this gives the opposing team less time to organize and mark the thrower's teammates and thus gives throwers and their teammates more time and room to get the ball back into play and under control.

Stationary throw-in

- Players should grip the ball by holding it with both hands spread behind and to the sides in a web effect, with fingers and thumbs spread as widely as possible.

- Feet can be either together, shoulder's width apart, or one foot in front of the other, whichever feels the most comfortable.

- The ball should be brought back behind the head with arms bent, so both the ball and the back of the hands are almost touching the back of the neck.

- Players should bend their trunk back according to how far they wish to throw the ball. They should also flex the knees slightly.

- Players throw the ball by simultaneously bringing the arms forward and over the head, straightening the arms, trunk, and legs. The weight of the body is transferred to the balls of feet, but care must be taken to ensure that both feet remain touching the floor.

Throw-in with a run up

The technique for a running throw-in is just the same as for a stationary throw-in, except a short run is included to help throw the ball farther. Some players may prefer to drag the back foot as the ball is released rather than put their weight on the balls of both feet. Care should be taken to judge the run (usually up to six yards) so the ball is released from behind the sideline and both feet remain on the ground.

THROW-IN DRILLS

138. BASIC THROW-INS

Organization:

Players hold their own soccer ball and stand on the sideline.

Purpose:

To teach players the correct technique for performing throw-ins

Procedure:

Players practice gripping the ball to the sides and behind using the W-webbed formation created by their hands. Players stand with both feet on the ground and behind the sideline while taking the throw-in. The ball is taken back behind the neck and then brought forward in one motion as the arms are straightened and the ball is released over and slightly in front of the top of the head.

Coaching points:

Coaches must ensure both feet remain firmly on the ground when the ball is released and both hands are used equally to perform the throw-in.

Variation:

Players take a short run up before throwing in order to throw the ball farther. Special care must now be taken to ensure both feet remain on the ground when the ball is released.

©2001 by Prentice Hall

139. THROWING THE BALL FARTHER

Organization:

Players hold their own soccer ball and stand about three yards behind the sideline.

Purpose:

To teach players the correct technique for performing long throw-ins

Procedure:

Players practice gripping the ball to the sides and behind it using the W-webbed formation created by their hands. Players run up while taking the ball back behind their neck and then bring it forward in one motion as the arms are straightened and the ball is released over and slightly in front of the top of the head.

Coaching points:

Coaches must ensure both feet remain firmly on the ground and behind the sideline when the ball is released and that both hands are used equally to perform the throw-in.

©2001 by Prentice Hall

140. DISTANCE THROW-INS

Organization:
Each player stands with a ball behind the sideline.

Purpose:
To practice throwing the ball as far as possible

Procedure:
Players either run all together or one at a time to the line and see how far they can throw the ball. Players then collect their balls to see who threw the farthest, and either return to the same line to try again or jog/sprint to a different touch-line if fitness is also an intended part of the drill.

Coaching points:
Players should be instructed that by taking a run up, bending their back farther backward, and bringing it forward faster along with the arms, they will be able to throw the ball a greater distance. Coaches must again ensure players keep both feet on the ground and behind the line from which they are throwing. If this rule is infringed upon during a game, the throw-in will be awarded to the opposing team.

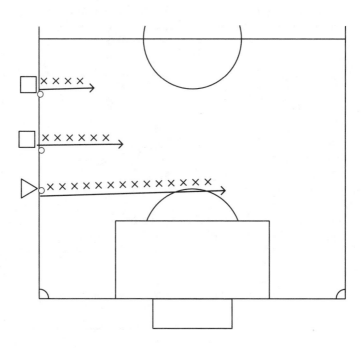

141. PASSING THE BALL STRAIGHT BACK
TO THE THROWER

Organization:

One thrower, one attacker, and one marker. One ball.

Purpose:

To practice passing the ball back to the unmarked thrower

Procedure:

Often during a game, all players will be marked up at a throw-in, and the throwers will have to decide how to best throw the ball back into play so their team keeps possession. If throwers are not marked by an opposing player, it is often a good idea for throwers to receive the ball straight back after throwing it into play so they can bring the ball under control and hopefully proceed to keep possession of the ball. During this drill, therefore, the throwers should throw the ball to their teammates who will control it and pass it back to the thrower, or even pass it back with their first touch to the thrower. The defenders will at first simply put pressure on the ball receivers so they must pass the ball back to the thrower as soon as possible, and then they should actually challenge for the ball as players become accustomed to the drill. Players must practice receiving balls on all the different parts of the body used for controlling the ball, including the foot, the thigh, the chest, and the head. This is because the defender will try to get to the ball first, so the receivers must move toward the ball. Although intended to land at their feet, the receiver may actually end up controlling it with the thigh, chest, or head before sending it back to the thrower.

©2001 by Prentice Hall

Coaching points:

Coaches should make sure players are not flat-footed; they should be on the balls of their feet. A quick move off the mark toward the ball can leave a defender a fraction of a second behind attackers, and can create the time needed to control the ball and pass it back to the thrower.

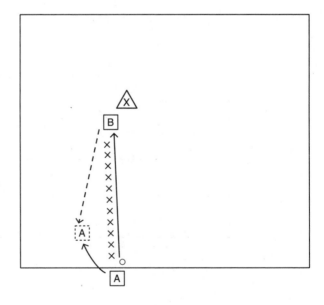

142. LONG THROWS IN THE ATTACKING THIRD OF THE FIELD

Organization:

Players organize themselves in and around the penalty box in a similar way to an attacking corner-kick.

Purpose:

To practice throw-ins in the attacking part of the field

Procedure:

If a team has players who can throw the ball a long way, a throw-in in the attacking third of the field can be used just like a set corner-kick, whereby instead of the ball being kicked toward the goal, the ball is thrown to this area. Many goal-scoring opportunities can be created from such a play. Throwers should aim toward their teammates positioned around the goal. Unless a player is clearly unmarked and can receive the ball at the feet to pass or shoot, the ball will often be thrown toward the player's head so he or she can either head the ball on goal or to another player. (Alternatively, the thrower may receive the ball back by throwing it short so the thrower can then cross the ball toward players near the goal.) This drill should at first be practiced with defenders who simply put pressure on the attacking team, and then, as attackers improve and become used to the drill, the defenders should challenge to try to win the ball.

Coaching points:

Coaches must ensure players do not stand still, but move around to lose their markers and find space in which to receive the ball.

©2001 by Prentice Hall

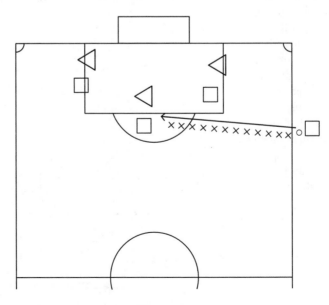

143. DEFENSIVE THROW-INS

Organization:

The defense has possession of the ball in his or her own half of the field.

Purpose:

To keep the ball away from the area where a dangerous counterattack can be initiated by the opposing team if he/she win possession of the ball

Procedure:

When a throw-in is taken in the defensive third of the field and all teammates are marked up, it is important to get the ball as far upfield as possible. This is usually done by throwing it as far down the sideline as possible, aiming for a teammate's head who can head it farther downfield with a flick on header (See page 132 to read about flick on headers.) It is important the ball is not thrown toward the center of the field if all players here are marked up, since from this area of the field a quick and dangerous counter attack can be created if the opposing team wins possession of the ball. Players must understand the central region in the defensive and middle third of the field are very dangerous areas in which to lose the ball to the opposition, since very quick break-away scoring opportunities can be created from there. It is, therefore, more desirable that a team lose possession of the ball on the flanks, so the opposition must work the ball back into the dangerous central region of the field before a goal-scoring opportunity can be created.

Coaching points:

Players must move around when receiving the ball from a throw-in so as to create space for themselves, and to create space for others by moving away and creating an area into which the ball can be thrown. If a player flicks the ball on with his or her head, other players must be prepared for this and move to receive the ball as it comes toward them, or move to a space where they anticipate the ball will land.

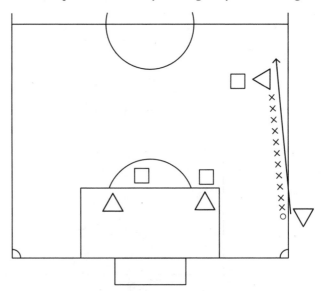

©2001 by Prentice Hall

144. CREATING SPACE AT THROW-INS

Organization:

Defense against attack or a regular scrimmage

Purpose:

To keep possession of the ball at a throw-in

Procedure:

Take throw-ins quickly before the other team has time to mark up. The thrower may not be able to do this, either because the ball traveled far out of bounds or the other team marks up quickly. Good communication between players is essential now. To get the ball back into play and keep possession, marked players must move around to lose their markers and find space to receive the ball. They can (1) move one step in one direction and quickly sprint in the other to create space; (2) move away to create a space for the ball and another player to move into; (3) throw the ball onto a player's head who then heads it into a space where another player is running to; or (4) unmarked throwers can receive the ball back.

Players who practice together often find these moves easier since they learn over time how and where each moves in certain situations. Build team communication at throw-ins with signals all teammates recognize. For example, bouncing the ball could mean the thrower will throw the ball to a player's feet as he or she moves into a space. The thrower cleaning the ball on the shirt could mean the ball will be thrown to a player's head to flick on to another player. Create signals during practice to make better setplays at throw-ins.

Coaching points:

Players must always move off the ball so players with the ball will have two or three passing options. This is true at *all* times during a game. Players without passing options usually lose the ball, and the team has to win possession again before starting a new attack. Watch during practice drills and scrimmages that players are alert and helping teammates. The thrower must try to take the throw quickly; teammates must be quick thinking and ready to receive the ball.

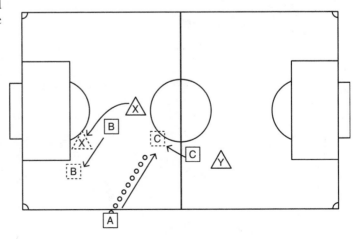

Section 7

HEADING

Section 7
HEADING

There will be many occasions in any game that a player must head the ball to shoot, pass, clear, or simply challenge an opposing player who is also attempting to head the ball, in the hope that the ball will find its way to a fellow team member.

Basic method and principles of heading

- The eyes must be kept open and the mouth shut when heading the ball. Players who close their eyes (a natural but wrong thing to do) invariably mishead the ball, or have the ball hit them in the face. If the mouth is not kept shut, players may bite their tongue.

- Players should use their forehead to head the ball. This is a very hard part of the head, and it will not hurt to head the ball there. This is also used because it gives the player the most accuracy and power when heading the ball.

Players put power into heading by not just allowing the ball to hit their head, but by snapping the neck and trunk into the ball, so they are using their whole upper body weight to head the ball. The head should also follow through the ball for maximum power.

Jumping to head the ball

Soccer is a fast and competitive game, and just as it is rare that players will have time to wait for a pass to arrive to them before opposing team members challenge, so it is with heading. Players must move to meet the ball, and with heading this means not standing and waiting for the ball to arrive at their head, but moving and jumping to challenge and win the ball in the air.

The jumping header involves the same basic principles as for any kind of header, in the respect that the eyes are kept open, mouth kept shut, the forehead is used to hit the ball, and the neck and trunk are used to put power into the header.

However, now the player must jump and meet the ball in the air. This involves a lot of skill in timing and judging the jump so the head reaches the high point of the jump at the same time the ball will be arriving. This judgment and timing have to be practiced and mastered, and can take a great deal of hard work.

Flick headers

A flick header is used to help the ball continue the way it is traveling. Flick headers can be extremely effective in passing the ball to team members at corner-kicks and throw-ins, or to send the ball into space for a team member to run on to. The flick header is performed by throwing the head back as the ball hits the forehead.

Redirecting the ball

The ball can be redirected when heading by hitting it on one side or slightly above or below its center. The same basic principles apply for heading the ball, except for the part of the ball with which the head makes contact. Redirecting the ball can also be achieved by allowing the ball to hit the forehead square on, and turning the head to one side or the other at the moment of contact. This also requires remarkably accurate timing and much practice.

Defensive headers often require the defender to simply head the ball far and clear of danger, and this is performed by heading the ball below the equator of the ball. Defensive headers should be directed wide toward the sidelines (or even out for a corner), and not into the dangerous central zone in front of the goal. For this reason it is important to be able to head both to the left and the right.

Offensive headers, especially when shooting on goal, require the player head the ball down toward the bottom corners of the goal. This is because it is more difficult for goalkeepers to save a shot directed to the ground than it is to save one coming to them at upper-body height. Offensive players will often receive balls on their head that have been crossed in from either side; therefore it is very important that attackers can redirect the ball coming from the sideline toward the goal. As the ball is contacted by the head, the player can achieve this by turning the trunk, neck, and head at the same time.

HEADING DRILLS

145. TEACHING PLAYERS TO BECOME USED TO HEADING A SOCCER BALL

Organization:

Each player has a soccer ball.

Purpose:

To help players get used to heading the ball

Procedure:

Players throw the ball in the air and then head it as it comes back down.

Coaching points:

Players must keep their eyes open and mouth shut when heading a soccer ball. Closing the eyes is the classic but understandable mistake among inexperienced players; players must watch the ball onto their forehead so it does not hit them in the face or on the nose.

Variation 1:

Players stand in pairs very close together to begin with, and one gently throws the ball to the other player who heads it back. As players improve, the ball should be thrown higher and from a farther distance. Players should also try to jump and head the ball as it arrives.

Variation 2:

Players stand in a circle around the coach who throws the ball to each player in turn so he or she can head the ball back.

146. BASIC HEADING

Organization:

Two players with one soccer ball

Purpose:

To help players get used to heading the ball

Procedure:

Players stand in pairs very close together to begin with, and one gently throws the ball to the other player who heads it back. As players improve, the ball should be thrown higher and from a farther distance.

Coaching points:

Players must keep their eyes open and mouth shut when heading a soccer ball. Players should also try to jump and head the ball as it arrives.

147. MORE BASIC HEADING

Organization:

Players stand in a circle around the coach who has one soccer ball.

Purpose:

To help players get used to heading the ball

Procedure:

The coach throws the ball to each player in turn so he or she can head the ball back.

Coaching points:

Players must keep eyes open and mouth shut when heading a soccer ball. Players should also try to move to the ball, and jump to head the ball as it arrives.

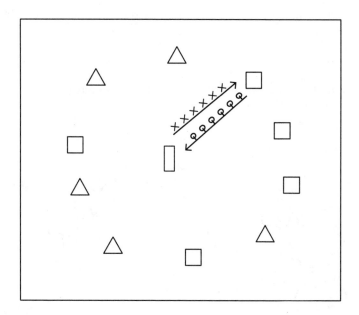

148. HEAD JUGGLING

Organization:

One player head juggles a ball in the air.

Purpose:

To develop personal skill as well as practice heading the ball correctly with the forehead

Procedure:

Players head juggle the ball to themselves to see how many repetitions they can achieve and to see how they improve with practice. Although this is a heading drill, if players drop their ball, they should be encouraged to continue juggling the ball with their feet and thighs to get the ball back up to their heads, rather than simply allowing the ball to fall to the ground and then picking it up again.

Coaching points:

Players must keep their eyes open and firmly fixed on the soccer ball to improve at this drill.

Variation:

Players perform the same drill, but this time with two or more players, so players are heading the ball to each other.

149. HEAD JUGGLING IN GROUPS

Organization:

Players divide into groups of three. Two players stand about 10 yards apart and one player stands between them.

Purpose:

To improve head juggling

Procedure:

Player A heads the ball to B, who heads the ball back to A, who heads it long to C, who heads it to B, who heads it back to C, who heads it long to A, and so on.

Coaching points:

Players should head the ball high to allow the receiving player time to move into a good position to head the ball on to the next player. Players should take turns at each position.

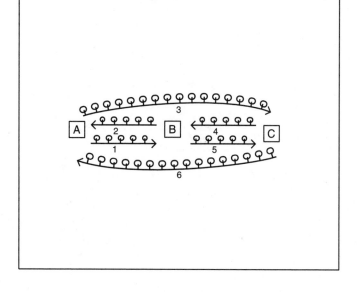

150. JUMP HEADERS ON GOAL

Organization:

Goalie in goal. Players line up at the edge of the penalty box. The coach has the soccer balls.

Purpose:

To encourage players to jump and head the ball

Procedure:

The coach serves the ball to a player running toward the goal who tries to head the ball into the goal.

Coaching points:

Players must move to the ball and jump to head it just as they would in a game; if players wait for the ball to arrive to their head, it will usually result in an opponent jumping and beating them to the ball. Offensive headers involve heading the ball low and hard toward the lower corners of the goal.

©2001 by Prentice Hall

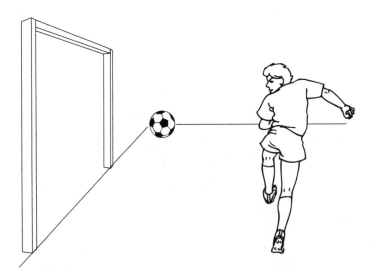

151. HEAD CATCH

Organization:

Players stand side by side facing the coach who has the one soccer ball to be used for the drill.

Purpose:

To get players used to heading the ball and reacting quickly

Procedure:

The coach throws the ball to each player in turn and calls out either "head" or "catch." However, "head" means catch in this game, and "catch" means head. Players sit down when they perform an incorrect action and the last player standing is the winner.

Coaching points:

Although this is a game for fun, players should still perform correct headers by using their forehead, keeping their eyes open and their mouths shut.

152. JUMP HEADERS WHILE MOVING BACKWARD

Organization:
Two players with one soccer ball.

Purpose:
To encourage players to jump and head the ball

Procedure:
The two players stand about 5 to 10 yards apart, and the server throws the ball to the receiver who must move toward the ball, judge its flight, and jump to head the ball back. The server moves toward the receiver, while the receiver moves backward so the receiver is jumping to head the ball while moving backward.

Coaching points:
This practice is very useful considering players often have to move backward and jump to meet a header during a game.

©2001 by Prentice Hall

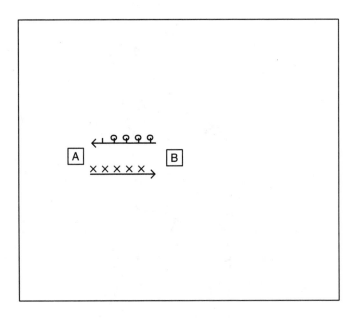

153. POWER HEADING

Organization:
Two players: One server, and one player sitting/lying down.

Purpose:
To practice putting maximum power into headers

Procedure:
Players heading the ball lie flat on their back, with the server standing two to three yards in front of them. As the server throws the ball, the receiver sits up to head the ball, snapping the neck and the momentum of the body weight as he or she sits up through the ball to give the header power.

Coaching points:
Players must snap the neck forward and through the ball as they head it. When they come to perform a regular header while jumping for the ball, this snap of the neck combined with the jump and bringing the whole upper body forward will add considerable power to the header.

154. MORE POWER HEADING

Organization:
Two players sit facing each other about three to six yards apart with one ball.

Purpose:
To practice putting maximum power into headers

Procedure:
Players head the ball to each other by each heading the ball out of their own hands.

Coaching points:
This drill encourages players to snap their neck through the ball to gain maximum power in the header.

155. HEADING AGAINST AN OPPONENT WHO IS ALSO CHALLENGING FOR THE BALL

Organization:

One ball server, one receiver facing the server about five yards away, and one opponent in front of the receiver, facing the server and away from the receiver.

Purpose:

To practice challenging against an opponent to win a head ball

Procedure:

The server throws the ball just over and just to one side of the opponent so the receiver must jump above the opponent to head the ball back. At first the opponent should not try to win the ball but simply jump with the receiver to make the header more difficult. However, as the drill progresses and the receiver gets used to someone jumping with him or her, the opponent should actually try to win the ball. Obviously good quality throws by the server are important to make this drill work well.

Coaching points:

Players must time their jump well so they meet the ball with their head when they are at the highest point of their jump. Players are not allowed to hold their opponent or use them to push themselves higher in their jump.

Variation:

The same drill as above except the receiver must sit down between each header. This acts as an excellent fitness as well as heading drill.

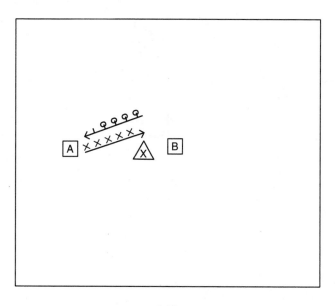

156. HEADER GOALS ONLY

Organization:

A regular small-sided or scrimmage game is played, where goals can be scored only from headers.

Purpose:

To encourage practice at crossing the ball into the penalty box to create head-scoring opportunities

Procedure:

A regular game is played except that goals can be scored only with the head.

Coaching points:

Players should play the ball wide so that crosses can be made into the penalty box. Attackers must make sure they move to receive headers and do not wait flat-footed for the ball to arrive at them.

©2001 by Prentice Hall

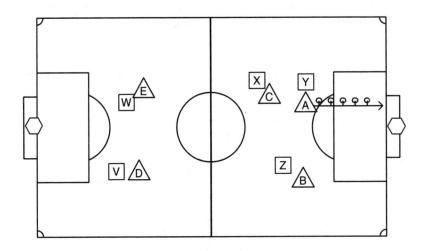

157. DEFENSE AGAINST ATTACKERS ON CORNER KICKS

Organization:

A regular corner kick is taken with the defense playing against the attackers.

Purpose:

To practice defending and attacking at corner kick situations

Procedure:

A corner kick is taken and kicked into the penalty box so defenders can try to head the ball away and the attackers can attempt to head the ball into the goal.

Coaching points:

Both defenders and attackers must move to and jump for the head ball. Defenders must clear the ball by heading it away to the flanks, while attackers must try to shoot on goal by heading the ball low and hard toward the corners of the goal. Kicks that are made towards the near post can be flicked on with a header for other players to head toward the goal. Obviously not every corner kick in this drill will end up in a goal being scored by a header; however, this is not important, and coaches must remind players that goals scored with any part of the body besides the hands and arms all count as goals. Just because a heading drill is being practiced, it does not mean players should not score with another part of their body if a header is not possible or suitable during any particular play.

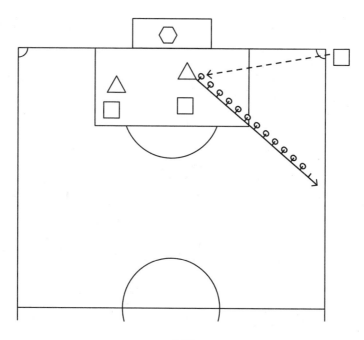

Section 8

GOALKEEPING

·Section 8

GOALKEEPING

This section will describe the basic elements of goalkeeping and outline some drills that will help players practice and improve playing at this position. The goalkeeping position in soccer is unique in that goalkeepers can use their hands as well as their feet to control the ball inside the penalty area. Goalkeeping is no simple task, as goalkeepers must be good with their hands, quick, decisive, brave, and have fast reflexes. All players make minor and major mistakes during any soccer game, and quite often these mistakes are missed by opponents or quickly repaired; however, if the goalkeeper makes a mistake it usually results in a goal, which can mean the difference between winning and losing a game. Goalkeepers must, therefore, practice extremely hard and should be well prepared mentally and physically for all games. They must accept that they will let goals in, and although some of these goals will be entirely their own fault, they must continue to play well and stay completely focused for the rest of the game.

The goalkeeper's stance

Just as field players stand in the ready position on the balls of their feet in order to be alert and able to move quickly off the mark, so goalkeepers should do the same. As well as standing in the ready position, goalkeepers must also have their hands in a ready position. Goalkeepers should stand with their legs shoulder's width apart, with knees slightly bent, and with the weight of their body on the balls of the feet. The hands should be at waist height, just outside the line of the body, with the palms of the hands either facing each other or out toward the ball.

Basic handling of the ball

The primary objective of the goalkeeper is to prevent the ball from going into the net by stopping the ball with the hands and catching it, if possible.

Handling ground shots

Shots that come toward the goalkeeper along the floor can be saved by either bending forward to scoop up the ball or kneeling to scoop up the ball.

BENDING TO SCOOP UP THE BALL

- Goalkeepers should keep their legs close enough together so if they miss the ball with their hands, it cannot pass between their legs.

- Goalkeepers should stand so they are facing the line of travel of the ball, and they should keep their eyes firmly fixed on the ball.

- Goalkeepers should bend their body at the waist, keeping their hands behind the ball, and cup it up to their chest while holding on to it tightly.

KNEELING METHOD

- Goalkeepers should stand facing the line of travel of the ball.

- Goalkeepers must keep their eyes firmly fixed on the ball.

- Goalkeepers must kneel down on one leg, making sure the knee touches the heel of the planted foot, to act as a barrier if the ball should pass between their legs.

- With their palms facing the approaching ball, goalkeepers scoop up the ball into their chest.

Catching waist-high and chest-high balls

- Goalkeepers stand and position themselves so they are facing the ball's line of flight.

- Goalkeepers must keep their eyes firmly fixed on the ball.

- The palms of the hands should be facing the ball.

- Goalkeepers must pull the ball tightly into the waist or chest.

Catching balls above the head

- Goalkeepers stand so they are facing the ball's line of flight.

- Goalkeepers must keep their eyes firmly fixed on the ball.

- Goalkeepers should spread their hands behind and to the sides of the ball (forming a W-webbed effect with their hands).

- Once the ball is caught, goalkeepers lower the ball and pull it tightly into their chest.

Positioning

The goalkeeper must be positioned correctly in relation to the goal and the position of the ball. As a rule of thumb, if the ball is to the left side of the goal, the goalkeeper must move toward the left; this is because the left near-post (i.e., the nearer post to the ball) is more vulnerable than the far post. If the ball is passed to the other side of the goal, the goalkeeper must adjust his or her position toward that side. The ball may well switch positions several times before a shot is taken, so goalies must continue adjusting their position to be prepared for the ball when it is eventually shot. When shifting positions in this way, goalkeepers must be able to move quickly from one side of the goal to the other without crisscrossing their legs as they move. Goalkeepers must always be in the ready position in case the shot is taken and they need to move sideways to position themselves in the line of the flight of the ball, or in case they need to dive in order to make the save.

Coming off the goal line

If an attacker is in possession of the ball and is dribbling unmarked toward the goal, the goalkeeper must come off the goal line in order to cut down the shooting angle of the attacker. To cut down the shooting angle means that as the goalie comes off the line, the shooting angle is closed down in the sense the goalkeeper will have less distance to dive in either direction to save a shot since the attacker will have less open goal at which to shoot.

Goalkeepers must be very decisive when deciding to leave the goal line. When they decide to come out, they must move quickly to the point they wish to get to and then assume the ready stance and prepare themselves to make the save. If goalkeepers get close enough to the player and the ball, they may decide to dive to save the ball. This does not mean they should dive forward to grab the ball, but dive lengthwise at the ball by dropping to their side and spreading their body in order to create a long obstacle that narrows the angle on goal even more for the shooting attacker.

The action of goalkeepers throwing themselves at the ball and the feet of the attacker who is about to shoot the ball takes a lot of courage, and this is one of the many essential attributes to being a good goalkeeper. Narrowing the angle is a very important goalkeeping skill and goalkeepers who simply remain on their goal line will give their opponents the maximum shooting angle. When novice goalkeepers first start to leave their goal line, they will need to look back to check exactly where they are in relation to the goal. However, practice will ensure that goalkeepers will no longer have to do this, but will be able to sense exactly where the goal is behind them.

Diving saves

Goalkeepers are often required to make diving saves when they do not have time to step across to position themselves in the line of flight of the ball. Diving saves, as with any save, require that goalkeepers are in the ready stance on the balls of their feet and can move quickly off the mark to dive for the ball and land on the side of their body. Although it is always preferable to catch the ball when performing a diving save or any other save, it is often impossible to do this and the goalkeeper must either punch or deflect the ball away from danger. Unless the ball can be punched or deflected a great distance from the goal, it is often safer to direct it out to a corner rather than to an awaiting attacker who may shoot and score the rebounded shot before the goal-keeper has time to get back on his or her feet and prepare to make another save. Goalkeepers should always remember that, if in doubt, they should be safe and put the ball out of play.

©2001 by Prentice Hall

METHOD FOR PERFORMING DIVING SAVES

- Goalkeepers must keep their eyes fixed firmly on the ball.

- Goalkeepers must take sideways steps toward the ball, and dive towards it when it is within reach.

- The ball should be caught if possible and pulled into the chest, otherwise punched or deflected to safety away from the goal.

Calling for the ball

Goalkeepers must consider their penalty area as a territory they must guard and take total control of. When the play is in this area, goalkeepers must verbally organize the other players, since they have the advantage of seeing the whole play in front of them and, therefore, only need to have a range of vision of 180 degrees. All the other play-ers must have a range of vision of 360 degrees, since they must know which players are in all directions throughout the game. The goalkeeper must instruct players where to stand and who to mark at corners and free kicks, as well as instruct defenders when to clear the ball out of danger. When goalkeepers call for the ball and prepare to catch or save it, all of their teammates must respect this call and leave the ball for the goal-keeper. The goalkeeper should use a loud, clear call, such as "keeper's ball." If goal-keepers do not call for the ball and one of their teammates tries to win the ball as well, the results can be disastrous; if the goalkeeper and a teammate challenge for the ball, they may set it up nicely for an attacker, who will have an open goal at which to shoot.

Goalkeeprs should also verbally instruct to their teammates even when the ball is not in and around the penalty area. They can see the whole field of play even when their team is up the field and should offer any helpful and necessary advice. This should illustrate how important it is that the goalkeeper understand all aspects of the game and not just the aspects of goalkeeping.

Building the attack from the goalkeeper

Once goalkeepers have the ball in their hands, they have a great advantage—they can either kick or throw the ball to a teammate, and no opposing player can take the ball from them while they are still holding the ball. It has been explained many times throughout this book that soccer is primarily concerned with ball possession and this is achieved by passing the ball to teammates until a goal-scoring opportunity is created. It is obvious, therefore, that goalkeepers must distribute the ball wisely when they have it in their hands. Goalkeepers can roll the ball out to a fullback, throw the ball out to someone farther away, or kick it far upfield toward an attacker. Different situations will always call for a different way of distributing the ball; for example, a quick long kick upfield can create a dangerous fast counterattack, whereas rolling the ball to a wide defender will allow a team to keep possession and to build up a slower attack.

GOALKEEPING DRILLS

158. CATCHING PRACTICE

Organization:

Two goalkeepers stand 5 to 10 yards apart with one ball between them.

Purpose:

To practice catching and handling the ball

Procedure:

The goalkeepers throw the ball to each other in order to practice catching the ball and pulling it tightly into their chest. The ball should be thrown so both players practice catching low balls, waist-high balls, and balls higher up (to and above their heads).

Coaching points:

Goalkeepers must move into the line of flight of the ball, get their body behind it, watch it closely as it comes toward them, and pull it tightly into their body.

159. REFLEX CATCHES

Organization:

Two goalkeepers stand facing each other at arm's length with one ball between them.

Purpose:

To practice reacting quickly when catching the ball

Procedure:

The player without the ball (player A) places hands on the partner's shoulders (player B), while the player with the ball (player B) holds the ball below player A's arms. Player B then drops the ball so that player A must catch it before it hits the ground.

Coaching points:

Goalkeepers must watch the ball closely and remain focused on saving and catching the ball.

160. REFLEX SAVES

Organization:

Two goalkeepers stand about five yards apart facing each other and with one ball between them.

Purpose:

To practice reacting quickly when saving the ball

Procedure:

One goalkeeper serves the ball with a firm kick or roll through the open legs of the other goalkeeper. As soon as the ball travels through the legs, the goalkeeper must turn and dive to save the ball.

Coaching points:

Goalkeepers must watch the ball closely and remain focused on saving the ball.

161. BENDING DOWN TO STOP AND SAVE A BALL TRAVELING ALONG THE GROUND

Organization:

Two goalkeepers stand about five yards apart with a soccer ball each.

Purpose:

To practice getting body behind the ball and scooping it tightly up into chest

Procedure:

The two goalkeepers roll the ball to each other at the same time, so they must either lean forward and scoop up the ball, or kneel down to collect the ball.

Coaching points:

Players should vary the speed and accuracy of the rolled balls. If the ball is not transferred directly toward them, goalkeepers must move into the line of flight of the ball. For slow traveling balls it is all right to lean forward and scoop the ball up. For faster traveling balls, however, it is important to bend down on one knee to save the ball, so the knee touches the floor and the heel of the other foot; this acts as a barrier in case the ball goes through the hands.

162. BENDING DOWN TO STOP AND SCOOP UP THE BALL

Organization:
Two goalkeepers stand about five yards apart with a soccer ball each.

Purpose:
To practice getting body behind the ball and scooping it tightly up into chest

Procedure:
One of the goalkeepers serves the ball by throwing it, while the other goalkeeper serves the ball by rolling it at the same time. They must either lean forward and scoop up the ball, or kneel down to collect the ball.

Coaching points:
Goalkeepers must again keep their eyes firmly fixed on the ball they intend to save, move into the line of flight of the ball, and get as much of their body behind the ball as possible in order to act as a barrier in case the ball is missed with the hands.

163. DIVING TO THE GROUND TO MAKE
LOW AND WIDE SAVES

Organization:

Two goalkeepers stand facing each other about 5 to 10 yards apart, with one ball between them.

Purpose:

To practice diving correctly and quickly to the ground

Procedure:

The goalkeepers roll or kick the ball wide of each other along the ground, so that diving saves must be performed in order to stop the ball.

Coaching points:

Goalkeepers must perform diving saves by diving sideways, watching the ball closely, using both hands to save and catch the ball if possible, and by landing on the side of the body while pulling the ball tightly into the chest. It is important that goalkeepers are alert and in the ready position on the balls of their feet, since many attackers will be able to shoot the ball accurately to the corners of the goal. This will require that goalkeepers take a few quick steps sideways before diving.

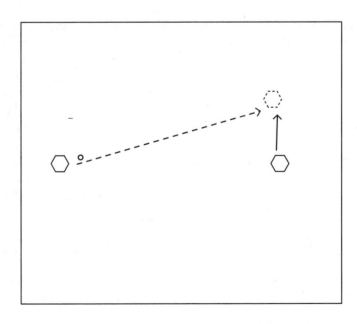

164. GOALKEEPERS MUST CONTINUE TO MOVE AND POSITION THEMSELVES IN RELATION TO THE POSITION OF THE BALL

Organization:

One goalkeeper stands in the goal, while three attackers stand 10 yards apart around the penalty box.

Purpose:

To practice adjusting their position as the ball moves from player to player out on the field

Procedure:

The three attackers pass the ball among themselves and shoot on goal after every 5 or 10 passes. Goalkeepers must constantly adjust their position in relation to the goal and the ball, so they are covering as much of the goal as possible, and so they will have to only dive or move a short distance in order to save any shots. For example, if the ball is with player A, the goalkeeper should move toward the left of the goal and move a yard or two off the goal line in order to cover the near post and cut down on the shooting angle to the far post. Similarly if the ball moves to player C, the goalkeeper should move toward the right side of the goal.

Coaching points:

Goalkeepers must move from side to side in a quick gliding motion and without crisscrossing their legs. They must always be alert and ready on the balls of their feet, so they can continue moving when necessary or even spring sideways to make a diving save.

©2001 by Prentice Hall

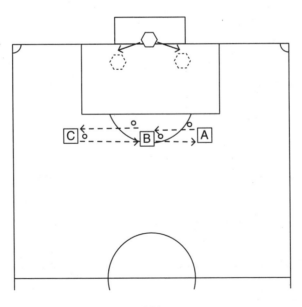

165. DEALING WITH HIGH BALLS

Organization:

One wide player crosses the ball toward a receiver, who heads or shoots the ball toward the goal and goalkeeper.

Purpose:

To practice coming off the line to save balls

Procedure:

The two attackers start at the halfway line and dribble toward the goal. As they get near to the penalty area, one player takes the ball wide to cross towards the other attacker who moves into the penalty box. As the cross comes over, the goalkeeper must judge the line of flight of the ball and move off the goal line in order to catch or punch it clear. The crossed balls should be in the form of both in-swinging and out-swinging crosses.

Coaching points:

Goalkeepers must be sure and decisive when they decide to leave their goal line in order to come out to save the ball. They must move out quickly and catch or punch the ball at the highest point possible in order to prevent attacking players from getting their head to the ball first. Goalkeepers should only punch the ball away when they do not feel they can safely catch it, and should use two-handed punches whenever possible since two-handed punches promote more power and accuracy than one-handed punches.

Variation:

The drill is set up as above with attackers heading or shooting crossed balls on goal except this time there are two attackers and two defenders in the penalty box. The goalkeeper must now decide whether it is possible to get to the crossed ball in order to save it, or whether to leave it for a defender to try to clear away because it's too far out. When goalkeepers do leave the goal line in order to come out for the ball, they must be sure to call out loudly "keeper's ball," so the defenders will not also attempt to win it.

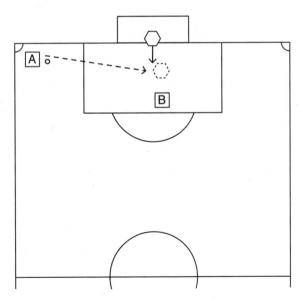

166. BACKPEDALING SAVES

Organization:

Players stand about 5 to 10 yards outside the penalty box, while the goalkeeper stands on the edge of the 6-yard box.

Purpose:

To practice saving shots chipped over the goaltender's head

Procedure:

One player at a time attempts to chip the ball over the goalkeeper who is off the goal line. The goalkeeper backpedals toward the goal as soon as the ball is kicked and attempts to either catch the ball or tip it over the crossbar.

Coaching points:

Goalkeepers will often find that when they are off their goal line, attackers will attempt to chip the ball over them and into the goal. Goalkeepers must be prepared for this, and always alert on the balls of their feet so they can move quickly backward in order to catch the ball, tip it around a goal post, or tip it over the crossbar. Goalkeepers must be able to sense exactly where the goal is behind them and how far they are away from it, since they will rarely have time to look and check on their bearings before making any saves.

©2001 by Prentice Hall

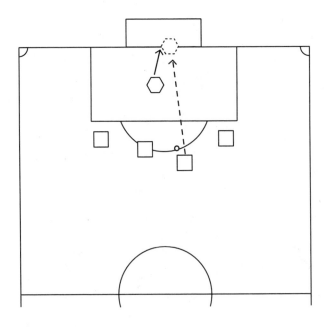

167. ONE ATTACKER AGAINST THE GOALKEEPER

Organization:

Players line up about 20 yards outside the penalty box and dribble toward the goal and goalkeeper in order to try to score.

Purpose:

To practice coming off the goal line to make saves

Procedure:

As the attacker dribbles close to the goal, the goalkeeper must come off the goal line in order to try to save the ball by cutting down the shooting angle of the attacker, or by diving at the feet of the attacker.

Coaching points:

Goalkeepers must first position themselves in line with the ball, and then decide whether to move off the goal line and toward the attacker with the ball. If the attacker is about to shoot the ball, goalkeepers should remain in the goal; if the ball is at too great a distance from the attacker to shoot immediately, goalkeepers must move quickly to the point where they wish to get and then assume the position ready to make the save. If there is time, goalkeepers should come all the way to the attacker and drop themselves sideways to the ground while trying to collect the ball. By dropping sideways to the ground and spreading the body, goalkeepers create a long barrier across the goal and narrow the shooting angle the attacker will have if the goalkeeper misses the ball while diving for it.

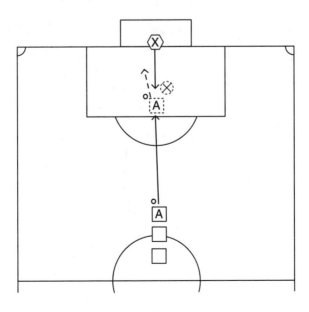

168. KICKING THE BALL UNDER PRESSURE

Organization:

A defender passes the ball back to the goalkeeper to kick up field, while an opposing attacker moves toward the ball and the goalkeeper in order to try to win it.

Purpose:

To practice kicking the ball

Procedure:

As the defender passes the ball back toward the goalkeeper, an opposing attacker moves toward the goalkeeper to put pressure on the ball. Goalkeepers must concentrate on watching the ball as they kick it with their first touch up the field.

Coaching points:

Goalkeepers cannot pick up the ball from a back pass unless it is headed, unintentionally passed to them, or chested back to them. For this reason, goalkeepers must be able to kick the ball accurately with their first touch. Defenders must be sure to make their back passes toward the sides of the goal in case the goalkeeper misses the ball. Goalkeepers will sometimes need to kick the ball clear when they leave the penalty box in order to get to the ball before an opposing breakaway attacker who is chasing a long pass that has cleared all the defenders. Goalkeepers should also practice their drop kicks and spot kicks during practice sessions, so as to be as accurate as possible during games when they kick the ball to their teammates.

©2001 by Prentice Hall

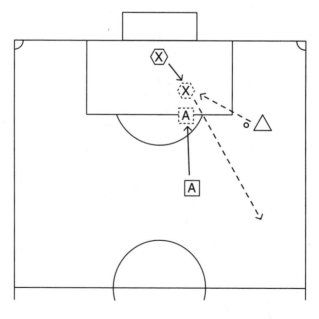

169. WORLD CUP

Organization:
Players divide themselves into pairs in one penalty box with a goalkeeper in the goal. Coaches stand at the edge of the penalty box with many soccer balls beside them.

Purpose:
To practice quick reflex saves

Procedure:
All the players enter the penalty box together, with each pair competing against all other pairs. The coach throws several balls into the penalty box at one time so players must attempt to win a ball and pass it back and forth to each other until they can shoot on goal. When a pair of players scores two goals, the pair leaves the penalty area, and the last pair left in the penalty area is eliminated. All pairs, except the one pair eliminated, return to the penalty area and the drill continues with one pair being eliminated at the end of each round until there is just one winning pair left. All shots on goal must be below waist height, and players may not shoot from inside the 6-yard box.

Coaching points:
Since there are many balls in play at any given time, goalkeepers must make quick reflex saves. If they need to make a diving save, they must get back to their feet as quickly as possible, while all the time watching the field of play and positioning themselves in line with the ball they expect to be shot next at goal.

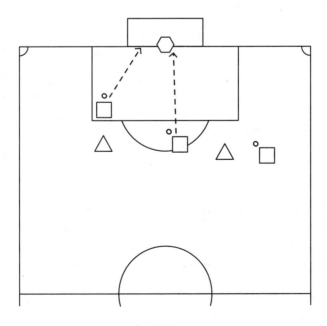

170. THROWING AND SAVING PRACTICE

Organization:

Two goals are set up about 20 yards apart and facing each other. One goalkeeper stands in each goal, with one ball between them.

Purpose:

To practice saving the ball
To practice throwing skills

Procedure:

The two goalkeepers try to score on each other by throwing the ball with pace and accuracy toward each other.

Coaching points:

In order to throw the ball accurately and with power, goalkeepers should use the over-arm throwing method. Goalkeepers position their body side on and in line with the player or area where they wish the ball to go. The ball is held in one hand with the wrist and arm curled around the ball. The ball is thrown by bringing the hand and arm over the shoulder and releasing the ball just past the vertical position.

©2001 by Prentice Hall

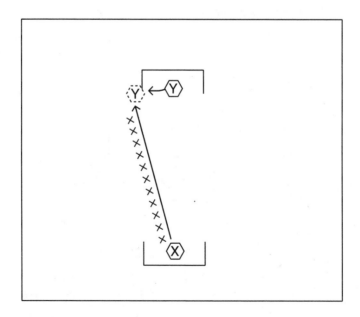

171. PENALTY SHOTS

Organization:

Players take penalty shots one at a time to see who can score the most goals without missing.

Purpose:

To practice facing penalty shots

Procedure:

Players take penalty shots one at a time. If they score, they continue to the next round; if they miss, they are eliminated.

Coaching points:

Although players are expected to score goals from penalties, goalkeepers will save penalty kicks from time to time, and it is a very good idea for them to practice such saves. Goalkeepers must remain on the goal line and may not move sideways until the ball has been struck. Penalty shot takers will either strike the ball as hard as they can, or they will try to place the shot more gently toward one of the corners. Whichever method is used, goalkeepers must be alert and poised on the balls of their feet, ready to dive toward one side. Goalkeepers must either guess or react to the side they expect the shot to go, and then watch the ball closely as they attempt to make the save.

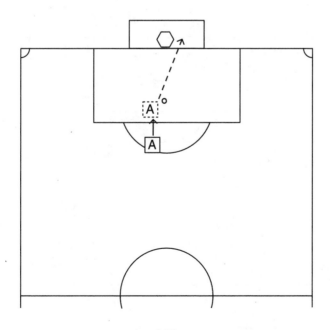

172. MOVING SIDEWAYS ACROSS THE GOAL

Organization:

One goalkeeper stands on the goal line, while another goalkeeper stands 5 to 10 yards away. One ball is needed between the two players.

Purpose:

To practice moving sideways from one side of the goal to the other with a sideways-bobbing motion whereby the legs do not cross over

Procedure:

The two goalkeepers move sideways together from one side of the goal to the other, while facing each other and throwing the ball to one another. Players must be sure to avoid crossing their legs as they move sideways, so they will always be ready to make a quick dive or change direction when necessary.

Coaching points:

Goalkeepers must be very nimble and quick-footed when moving around their goal and positioning themselves in line with the ball. When the ball is saved and caught during a game, it should be pulled tightly into the chest to prevent it from being knocked free by opponents.

©2001 by Prentice Hall

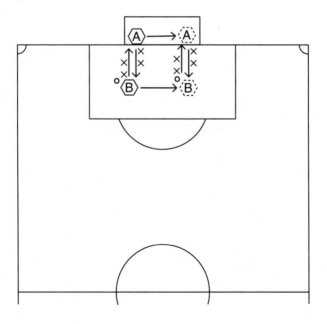

173. QUICK SAVES IN SUCCESSION

Organization:

All players have a ball at their feet and form a circle around the goalkeeper, so that all players are about 5 to 10 yards away from the goalkeeper.

Purpose:

To help goalies be alert and quick on their feet so they can constantly change positions and get in line with the next ball being shot.

Procedure:

Players shoot/kick the ball at the goalkeeper one at a time. The goalkeeper saves and catches the ball before rolling the ball back to the kicker and turning to face the next player.

Coaching points:

Goalkeepers must reposition themselves as fast as possible after each shot so they are ready for the next shot. Goalkeepers often make saves in a game where they do not catch the ball and must be able to prepare quickly for any rebounded saves that fall at the feet of attackers.

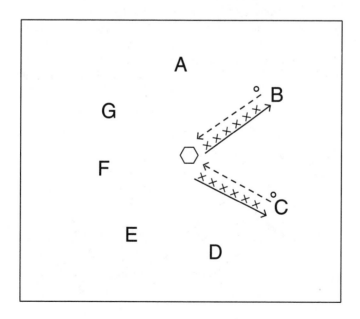

174. HIGH AND WIDE SAVES

Organization:

Goalkeepers sit on the ground while the coach/server throws the ball high and wide for them to catch.

Purpose:

To practice reaching to catch high and wide balls

Procedure:

While the goalkeeper remains sitting on the ground, the coach serves the ball high and wide to one side and then the other, so the goalkeeper must lean and reach toward the sides in order to catch the ball.

Coaching points:

Goalkeepers must be able to reach and stretch for balls that are wide of them, since it is always preferable to catch and hold as many wide shots as possible, rather than just getting their fingertips on the ball and directing it out of bounds for a corner.

Variation:

The goalkeeper stands in the goal while the coach serves high and wide balls quickly towards the right, then to the left, then to the right again, and so on. Goalkeepers must be alert on the balls of their feet so they can move quickly toward the ball and dive to make all the wide saves; they must also get back to their feet quickly after each save and prepare themselves for the next served ball. The coach should gradually make the serves wider and should vary the height of the ball so that some serves are high and some low.

175. SAVING A SHOT AND THEN PREPARING QUICKLY TO SAVE ADDITIONAL SHOTS

Organization:

Players have their own ball and line up side by side just outside the penalty box so they can shoot at the goal.

Purpose:

To practice making many saves in succession

Procedure:

The player at one end of the line shoots at the goal. As soon as the ball has either been saved or gone into the goal, the next player shoots a ball, and so on, until all players have taken a shot at goal.

Coaching points:

Goalkeepers must make each save quickly before positioning themselves for the next shot. Like many drills, this acts as an excellent fitness drill for goalkeepers. Goalkeepers should perform the exercise once through and then rest while the next goalkeeper takes a turn in the goal.

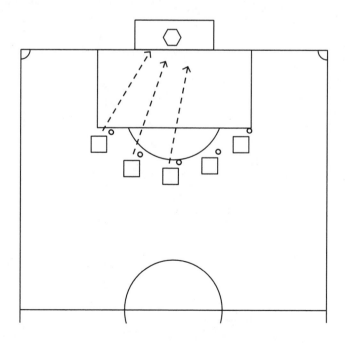

176. ONE GOALKEEPER FACING SHOTS FROM BOTH SIDES OF THE GOAL

Organization:

Either a goal is made from cones, or a goal with no net is used, so the goalkeeper can face shots from both sides of the goal.

Purpose:

To practice turning from one direction to the other to be in position for many quick shots taken in succession.

Procedure:

A player from line A dribbles toward the goal and shoots on goal before collecting the ball and dribbling around the goal to the end of line B. Meanwhile, as soon as this player is about to shoot, the first player from line B starts to run toward the goal and shoots on goal before collecting the ball and dribbling to the back of line A.

Coaching points:

Goalkeepers must make the save and then quickly turn and position themselves for the next shot. Although most field players will never play in goal during a game and most goalkeepers will never play out on the field, it is a very good idea to have players switch roles from time to time during practice. This will help goalkeepers to understand what playing other positions entails and should give them an idea of what attackers are thinking when they are attempting to score. This kind of exercise will not only help goalkeepers to improve their goalkeeping skills, but will also help the coach to discover any potential backup goalkeepers for the future.

©2001 by Prentice Hall

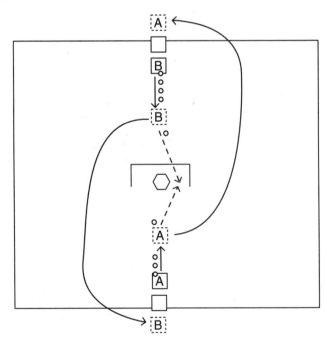

Section 9

TACTICS AND POSITIONS

Section 9
TACTICS AND POSITIONS

General tactics

The use of the word "tactics" in soccer can be very misleading. Many teams will say they play using certain tactics and these tactics determine whether or not they are successful. This can be true to a certain extent; for example, a team may use the tactic of passing the ball wide to a player who runs to the end line and crosses the ball to a player in the penalty box to kick into the goal. However, the word tactics has a very broad meaning. Everything that has been described and taught in this book is a tactic. For example, the idea of kicking the ball high or low, throw-ins, and marking opponents are all tactics. Tactics refer to the most simple of skills from such things as dribbling the ball, to the most advanced skills such as fake runs to create space for other teammates.

Probably the best piece of advice in deciding what tactics to use in soccer is to keep the play simple. Coaches must see what players do effectively and poorly as individuals and as a team and they must build upon and use the skills, tactics, and plays players perform well together as a team. The team that plays a simple passing game with all teammates moving and supporting each other off the ball will invariably beat the team of "superstars" that does not pass, but instead has each player try to beat the opposing team and score themselves.

The following is a list of commonly used tactics coaches instruct their team to use in order to keep the play simple and effective:

- Pass the ball whenever possible (this is frequently referred to as allowing the ball to do the work).

- All players must know the role and duties associated with their positions.

- Players must play with their heads up so they have good vision of all players and space around them.

- Players must take as many shots as possible; the rule of thumb for shooting is to shoot the ball whenever possible, but to shoot only if there are no other players in a better scoring position.

- Players must follow up on all shots in order to take advantage of any rebounds.

- Players should try to shoot low and hard toward the corners of the goal.

- Teams should try to take throw-ins as quickly as possible.

- The defense must move up together and quickly when their team is attacking or when they have cleared the ball upfield.

- Midfield players must play both defense and offense.

- Only one player from a team should compete for the ball at any given time, while all other players should be in good positions to receive the ball.

Scrimmages

Being successful at soccer, as with most sports, requires that players individually learn and practice all the basic skills and then put these skills together and use them in the real game situation. It is very important, therefore, that scrimmages are used in practice sessions.

Systems of play

Every soccer team will use a system of play according to the number of defenders, the number of midfielders, and the number of attackers used, and the system will be described in that order (e.g., 4, 4, 2 or 4, 3, 3).

    Players should be able to perform the basic soccer skills well in both a defensive and an offensive role since soccer is a very fast game and players can never be sure when they may find themselves in a different position from the one in which they are playing; for example, defenders may find themselves in the opposing penalty area with a cross coming over that needs to be kicked into the goal; or center forwards may find they have to come back to help out on defense and must jockey or tackle an opposing forward who is about to score. Players should try playing in other positions during practice, since this will help them out when they find themselves temporarily in a different position during a game. It will also help players when they try to beat their opponents in games, since they will have played their opponents' position during practice and will understand better what the position entails and what their opponents will be thinking as they both challenge for the ball.

Positions

Defenders

Although all players in a team must defend when the opposing team has the ball, it is the actual defenders who form the last line of players before the goal and goalkeeper. It is these players who must either win the ball, kick it up field, or kick it out of bounds if a scoring opportunity by the opposing team is to be avoided. Midfielders and attackers defend in the sense that they track back toward their own goal and mark the opposing team when they are in possession of the ball; however, they do not usually go so far back as the defenders, since once the ball is won by the defense, the midfielders and attackers must be prepared for the counterattack.

When the opposing team is in the attacking third of the field and attempting to create a goal-scoring opportunity, it is essential that defenders keep close to the players they are marking. One of the most important things for defenders to remember is to always stay goal side of the ball and other opposing attackers. This means defenders should never have the ball or opposing attackers between themselves and their goal. Defenders must never leave the player they are marking to go forward to tackle the player with the ball. They must be goal side of the ball and the player they are marking, even when the player they are marking does not have the ball.

It is fine for defenders to push forward during an attack, but they must get back to their position as quickly as possible when the play is over, and it is essential that a midfielder cover the defender's position while the defender is involved in the attacking play.

Defenders, like all other players, must be in good shape to play soccer. Not only do they need to chase and track opponents with and without the ball, but they must also move up the field after a defensive play has been made and the ball has been moved up to the opponent's half of the field. The defenders must move up the field together in a line so any opposing players who remain in their half will be offside if the ball is played back to them quickly. Players are offside if the ball is passed forward to them and they do not have two players (including the goalkeeper) between themselves and the goal line. Players cannot be offside if they are in line with the last defender; if they receive the ball directly from a throw-in, a corner kick, or a goal kick; or if they are in their own half of the field. Therefore, since players cannot be offside in their own half, defenders should not move up further than their halfway line.

Attackers

Attackers, or forwards as they are also known, are offensive players and usually score most of the goals. Attackers are fast players who can dribble, shield, pass, and shoot the ball well. Attackers must learn to move off the ball just like all other players on the field. If they stand still and wait for the ball to come to them, they will make it easy for opposing defenders to mark them and win the ball. Attackers should constantly move around to try to lose and confuse their markers as well as to find a space where they will be free to receive a pass. Forwards must be encouraged to shoot as much as possible, since there will be no goals scored without shots. Although forwards should spend much time during practice on finishing and shooting so they may convert as many scoring opportunities as possible into goals during games, forwards who miss goals during games should not be criticized; instead they should be encouraged to keep trying. The rule of thumb for shooting is that if players are within range of the goal and can shoot, they should; if they need to beat two or three players, they should pass the ball if there are passing options available. If they have no teammates in a better scoring position, or no support from teammates, they should use their dribbling ability and fakes to try to beat the defenders and score themselves. Forwards should also remember that although they will rarely have much time to control and shoot the ball when they are in front of the goal, due to pressure from opposing defenders, there will be times when they find themselves all alone. In these situations they must stay composed and take time to control and shoot the ball well.

Defenders will soon learn which opposing attackers use only one foot to dribble and shoot and will find it much easier to mark and tackle them. It is very important, therefore, that all soccer players kick with both feet, no matter what position they play. Most players will have a preferred foot that they use to kick, but they must also be prepared to kick with their weaker foot when necessary. If, for example, left-footed attackers have a clear shot on goal, but the ball is close to their right foot, they must be able to use the right foot rather than take time to bring the ball to the left foot. If they take too long to shoot, they may be tackled by a defender and miss out on a very good goal-scoring opportunity. The only way to get better at kicking with the weaker foot is to practice using it as often as possible.

Midfielders

Midfielders are the players who play between the defenders and attackers. They are usually the best "all-rounded" players on the team, since they are involved in defense and offense. When their team is in possession of the ball, they help with the attacking play and must be good at dribbling, passing, and shooting. When their team loses the ball, they must help on defense and must be good at tackling and marking. Since midfielders play both offense and defense they must also be strong and fit. If the attack breaks down and the opposing team makes a counterattack, they must recover quickly to help their defense; the next minute their defense may win the ball back and the midfield must then move upfield to help the attackers again. The possession of the ball changes constantly between teams in soccer and the midfielders must be able to read the game and be well prepared for this so they are not constantly caught out of position.

Although midfielders attack and score goals, they must always be prepared to defend more than attack. Their primary duty is to win the ball either at midfield or in the defensive zone and help build an attack by passing the ball to the forwards, and then support the attack by giving the attackers passing options back, or by moving into a position where they might receive a pass and shoot on goal. Since midfielders play between the defense and attack of both teams, they must have excellent vision of all players around them; they will constantly have teammates and opposition players in front, behind, and to both sides. If they receive a pass, they must know how much time they will have on the ball and whether they can turn or whether they must pass off the ball quickly to another teammate. It is very important the ball is not lost in the middle third of the field, since counterattacks from this area can be dangerous and very costly.

TACTICAL AND POSITIONAL DRILLS

177. LOOKING FOR SPACE

Organization:

Players are divided into two teams and position themselves on one half of the field. The coach has the soccer ball.

Purpose:

To teach players to spread out and move to some space in which to receive a pass

Procedure:

The coach stands at the halfway line and blows the whistle to indicate that attacking players must move around and find space in which to receive the ball, while their opponents move with them to mark them as tightly as possible. The coach passes the ball to a player who has moved to a good position and has found a good space in which to receive the pass.

Coaching points:

Players must move quickly off the mark in order to receive a pass. After the coach passes the ball to a well-positioned player, all players must stand still so the coach can comment on each player's position.

©2001 by Prentice Hall

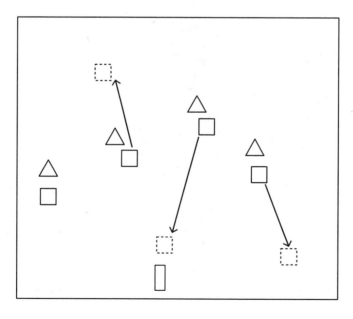

178. PRACTICE STANDING IN THE READY POSITION

Organization:

Players stand about five yards apart facing the coach.

Purpose:

For players to become used to standing on the balls of their feet and being alert

Procedure:

Players stand with their legs about shoulder's width apart and with one leg slightly forward of the other. With a blow of the whistle, the coach points either forward, backward, left, or right. All players must move about five yards in that direction, assume the ready position again on the balls of their feet, and wait for the next whistle and direction.

Coaching points:

Players need to be very quick off the mark when playing soccer. Offensive players will need this skill to beat defenders, and defensive players will need it to keep up with and beat attackers to the ball.

Variation:

The drill is set up as above, except each player has a soccer ball. This drill is an excellent way to encourage players to keep their heads up and focused, rather than to look down at the ball and their feet. Players must be able to dribble and move with the ball while sensing rather than looking at it all the time. This is so they can be aware where teammates and opponents are positioned.

179. FURTHER PRACTICE AT STANDING IN THE READY POSITION

Organization:

Any regular practice drill or scrimmage game is played.

Purpose:

To help players learn to always be on the balls of their feet when playing soccer

Procedure:

Coaches must ensure that players are never standing flat-footed when involved in the play. Therefore, during practice sessions, coaches should look for occasions when players are easily beaten by opponents because they are not ready and alert to move to the ball quickly.

Coaching points:

Coaches should use their whistle to instruct players to stop the play and stand exactly where they are. By doing this, coaches can point out to the whole team why certain players are standing in good positions while other players are not. Players will realize exactly why they are doing certain things wrong, and will not only consciously try to amend them, but will also unconsciously try to do so due to the fact that they know the whistle will blow and the game will stop whenever errors occur.

180. JOCKEYING OPPONENTS

Organization:

One player dribbles toward the goal and a defender who is positioned outside the penalty box.

Purpose:

To practice jockeying players with the ball until the time is right to tackle

Procedure:

As the player with the ball approaches the defender, the defender must jockey the player to one side by angling the body and forcing the player in one direction. This will make the eventual tackle easier, since the defender will have forced the player to go one way, rather than allow the player to run straight and choose whether to go either left or right. As the player with the ball moves on to beat the defender and head toward the goal to shoot, the defender must time and execute the tackle.

Coaching points:

Defenders must be alert and ready on the balls of their feet so they can react quickly to the attacker's fakes and fast moves. Defenders must learn to watch for their opponent's habits during a game; this may mean giving extremely fast opponents an extra yard or so, forcing players to move onto the side of their weaker foot, or recognizing the particular fakes and dribbling patterns of certain opponents. Fullbacks should always jockey opponents toward the sidelines away from the central area of the field where the opponent's shooting angle and passing options to teammates in goal-scoring positions would be most dangerous.

©2001 by Prentice Hall

181. DEFENDERS MARKING THEIR OPPONENTS TIGHTLY FROM BEHIND AS THEY RECEIVE THE BALL

Organization:

One server passes the ball to a receiver on the edge of the penalty box who has a defender marking tightly from behind. A goalkeeper is in the goal.

Purpose:

To prevent attackers from turning with the ball

Procedure:

Defenders mark the attackers very closely (about an arm's length away) as they receive the ball to prevent them from turning and shooting on goal. The defender must be sure to watch the ball and not be fooled by the fakes the attacker will be using to try to find space and shoot the ball on goal. If the attacker does turn, the defender must time and carry out the tackle to prevent the attacker from shooting and scoring. If attackers feel that defenders are marking them so tightly that they cannot turn with the ball, they should pass the ball back to the server and move away to find space in which to receive another pass.

Coaching points:

Defenders must be alert so they can move with and continue to tightly mark the attacker goal side, and hopefully prevent them from turning with the ball. Defenders should also try to read and intercept passes from the server if possible; however, if defenders do decide they can win the ball before the pass reaches the receiver, they must be absolutely sure they will get to the ball first and not allow the receiver to have a free run at goal by missing the interception.

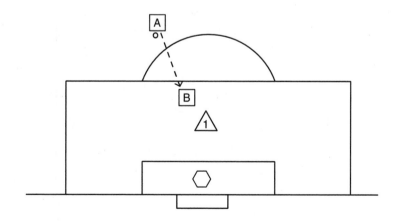

182. DEFENSE VERSUS ATTACK WITH DEFENSE ATTACKING ONE GOAL AND ATTACKERS ATTACKING TWO GOALS

Organization:

The drill is set up using one half of the field and three goals.

Purpose:

To use good vision, with attackers switching their attack from one goal to another, and defenders reading this switch and covering all players

Procedure:

Attackers must use space when attacking, and this can be achieved in this drill by suddenly switching the attack from one goal to the next. Defenders must cover both goals and, although they should be closer to the goal the opposing team is attacking at that moment, they must be aware of opposing players at the other goal in case the attacking play is suddenly switched to that goal.

Coaching points:

Sweepers should benefit greatly from this drill, since they are in effect covering two goals at once. Although all defenders must read and be aware of how the play may change and where opposing players are positioned, the sweeper should be verbal in communicating with and organizing the rest of the defense. Defenders must understand how to split two attackers and mark them both simultaneously. This means standing closer to the one who is closer to the ball and the play, while at the same time dropping off far enough goal side of the other player so that, should the ball be passed to this player, the defender will have time and space to recover and mark them.

©2001 by Prentice Hall

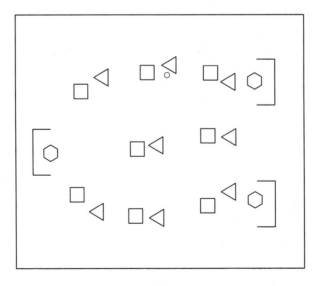

183. TWO TEAMS VERSUS ONE IN AND AROUND A GRID

Organization:

Three teams: two inside the grid and one outside along the lines.

Purpose:

To practice wall passes and creating good passing angles

Procedure:

The two teams inside the grid play against each other and score a goal by making 10 consecutive passes. The team with possession of the ball may use the players standing on the outside of the grid to play wall passes to.

Coaching points:

The team with possession of the ball inside the grid must constantly be moving off the ball in order to create good passing options and angles for the player on the ball.

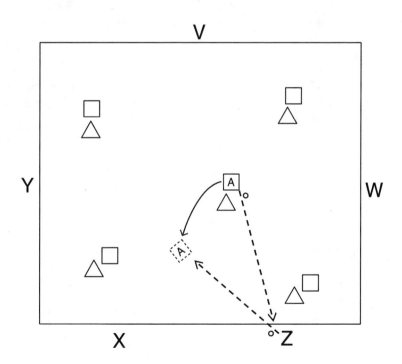

184. RECEIVING THE BALL WITH AN OPPONENT MARKING CLOSE BEHIND

Organization:

One server, one receiver, and one defender.

Purpose:

To practice receiving a pass and passing it back to a teammate with a first-time pass

Procedure:

The server passes the ball to teammates who are about 10 to 15 yards away and who have a defender marking them tightly from behind. The receiver of the pass must move to meet the ball and pass it back first time to the server. At first the defender should simply stick very close to the receivers to put pressure on them, but as the receivers improve at passing the ball back with their first touch, the defender should actually attempt to win the ball.

Coaching points:

The receiver of the ball must be alert and move quickly off the mark to come to meet the ball. In order to pass the ball back first time, players must watch the ball carefully onto the foot as they kick it. Servers of the ball must ensure their passes are firm enough to reach the receiver quickly to prevent the defender having time to intercept the ball, but not so hard that the receiver has difficulty in controlling and passing the ball back in one movement.

Midfielders will often receive the ball when they are marked very tightly, and although they may sometimes attempt to turn and beat their marker, they must also be well practiced at playing the ball off first time to open teammates.

©2001 by Prentice Hall

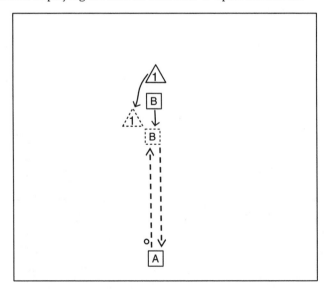

185. USING GOOD VISION

Organization:

Two servers about 20 yards apart with an attacker and a defender between them.

Purpose:

To practice looking up as much as possible to see what and who is around them, and especially doing so before looking down to control the ball as a pass is coming toward them

Procedure:

Attackers must look to see how far the defender is behind them as they move to receive and control the ball being passed to them by one of the servers. Defenders should vary how close they are to the attackers, so that if attackers see they are several yards behind them, attackers should control the ball, turn with it, and attempt to beat the defender before passing the ball to the opposite server. If defenders are marking attackers closely, on the other hand, attackers must look and see this as they are about to receive the ball, so they know to pass the ball straight back to the server, and move quickly off to lose the defender and find space where they can receive the ball again and hopefully turn with it.

Coaching Points:

Players must get used to playing with their heads up as much as possible and not watching the ball for too long as they control and dribble it. It is a very common error for beginning and inexperienced players to receive the ball and not know who is around them, where their free teammates are positioned so they can pass to them, or how much time they have, if any, to control the ball and turn with it before an opponent arrives to tackle them. Players should constantly look around to see where teammates and opponents are positioned, even when they do not have the ball. When the ball is coming toward them, they should look up and take a "mental snapshot picture" of what is around them; although other players will have changed their position by the time the receiving players have brought the ball under control, this "mental snapshot picture" will save the receivers vital seconds when they have the ball at their feet, since they will not have to look up and decide what to do next with the ball, but will already have a good picture in their mind of what they will do. They may play the ball off first time to a player whose position they will already know from their "mental snapshot picture," they may control the ball and turn with it to dribble, or they may control the ball and then know that they have time to look up to find another passing option.

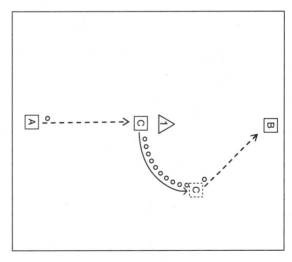

186. A WALL PASS INTO SPACE BEHIND THE OPPONENT

Organization:

One server (the left fullback in this example), one receiver (the left midfielder in this example), and one opponent marking the left fullback.

Purpose:

To practice passing the ball back to the defense and then moving away from their opponent into a space where they can receive a pass down the sideline to begin the attack

Procedure:

After receiving the ball from the goalie, the left fullback $\boxtimes$ passes the ball to the left midfielder $\boxed{B}$. The left midfielder is tightly marked by the opposing right midfielder $\boxed{1}$, so the left midfielder passes the ball first time back to X. The midfielder then moves away to the inside of $\boxed{1}$ and heads out to the wing and past $\boxed{1}$ to receive a second pass from X into this wide attacking position.

Coaching points:

The effectiveness of this move depends largely upon how well players are marked by their opponents; it becomes important, therefore, that players practice performing this move as quickly as possible, to prevent their opponents having enough time to mark them tightly. After the left fullback has made the second longer and wide pass to the left midfielder, the left fullback, along with other teammates, must support the left midfielder who has the ball.

©2001 by Prentice Hall

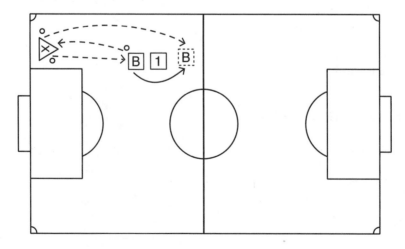

187. ADJUSTING TACTICS ACCORDING
TO THE CONDITIONS

Organization:
Teams practice playing on fields of different sizes and with different surfaces.

Purpose:
To understand that their system and style of play may have to vary from game to game.

Procedure:
Players must appreciate that different styles of play will be required on different sized fields in order to achieve success. For example, teams will often play a 4, 3, 3 system on a very narrow field, and a 4, 4, 2 system on a wider field. This is because using three midfielders and three attackers on a narrower field will allow players to spread out and make more use of what little space exists. It is important, therefore, that teams practice playing on different sized fields during training. This is particularly important when a team knows they will be playing a game on a field vastly different in shape or size from the one to which they are accustomed.

Players and teams must also be able to adjust to the different kinds of surfaces they will play on (for example, a bumpy surface, a flat surface, an artificial surface, a dry surface, or a wet surface), as well as the various climactic conditions under which they will play (for example, wet conditions, dry conditions, hot conditions, cold conditions, or windy conditions).

Coaching points:
No matter what conditions they are playing under, players must concentrate on playing the game simply as a team. For example, windy conditions will require the ball be kept on the ground as much as possible, narrow fields will require players pass the ball two-touch as much as possible, and wet conditions will require players take care they are not caught flat-footed if balls skid quickly past them.

188. A SCRIMMAGE GAME

Organization:

Eleven versus eleven, eight versus eight, five versus five, etc.

Purpose:

To practice putting all skills and tactics together in a game-like situation and to ensure that players are match fit

Procedure:

Scrimmage games are an excellent way for players to practice playing together as a team. For example, defenders must get used to playing together as a unit and moving out of defense together after the ball has been cleared, or when they are playing the offside trap. During the scrimmage the coach can instruct one team to push extra players forward so the other team must practice bringing extra players back on defense. Players can practice attacking and defending at throw-ins, corner kicks, and free kicks.

Coaching points:

The coach must use scrimmages to fine-tune and prepare players for real games. Players must support and help each other to keep possession of the ball, and must be able to read the game and adjust to any strengths and weaknesses of the opposition. The coach should blow the whistle to indicate that players stop the play during scrimmages and stand where they are; this gives the coach the opportunity to offer advice on particular plays, and to demonstrate which players are and are not in good positions.

189. THROW UP

Organization:

All players have their own ball except for one player.

Purpose:

To practice trapping the ball quickly

Procedure:

When the coach blows the whistle, all players throw their ball in the air and must trap any ball except their own. The one player who does not trap a ball is eliminated and sits out. The coach now removes one more ball from the game so every round has one more player than balls. The last player left is the winner.

Coaching points:

Players should use good vision to decide which ball they will trap and must move quickly to the ball to bring it under control.

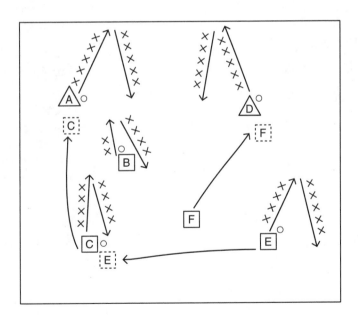

190. BUILDING THE ATTACK FROM DEFENSE

Organization:

The fullback receives the ball from the goalkeeper and passes the ball upfield to teammates.

Purpose:

To build the attack from the back and keep possession of the ball

Procedure:

The fullback receives a pass from the goalkeeper and plays the ball forward, either with a short pass to a midfielder moving toward the ball, or with a longer pass to an attacker. Fullbacks should get used to automatically moving wide to the sidelines when their goalkeepers have the ball, so that they may receive the ball from them. Goalkeepers will tell players to move up if they wish to punt the ball upfield themselves, but fullbacks should initially move wide as quickly as possible to build a fast attack from the back if they receive the ball.

Coaching points:

If the fullbacks receive the ball wide from the goalkeeper and have no passing options forward, they should not be afraid to pass the ball square to their sweeper who can then pass the ball out to the other sideline in the hope that an attack can be built down that side. However, players should not pass the ball around in the defense if the opposing team is close by and could move forward to tackle the ball; if no passing options are available, the ball should be cleared by kicking it long up the field.

©2001 by Prentice Hall

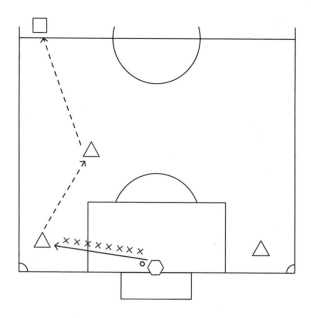

191. DEFENSIVE CLEARANCES

Organization:

An attacking wide forward dribbles the ball to the endline and crosses the ball toward the penalty area, where there are two teammates waiting to score, and where there are also two defenders.

Purpose:

To practice winning and clearing the ball away from the penalty area, where potential goal-scoring opportunities are often created

Procedure:

The two defenders must mark the two central attackers who are waiting to receive the crossed ball to score. The defenders must be ready and alert so they can be first to the ball when it is crossed, and so they can then clear it upfield or to a free teammate nearby.

Coaching points:

Defenders must either head the ball high and wide to clear it, or kick it long and wide; they must ensure the ball is not simply headed or kicked to just outside the penalty area, a position from where the opposing team could take a quick shot on goal. Defenders must not be afraid of clearing the ball out of play for a throw-in or corner, since it is always better to give possession of the ball to the other team in this manner than it is to give up a goal or an immediate goal-scoring opportunity; as the opposing team collects the ball to take the throw-in or corner kick, the defending team will have time to organize and mark the opposing players.

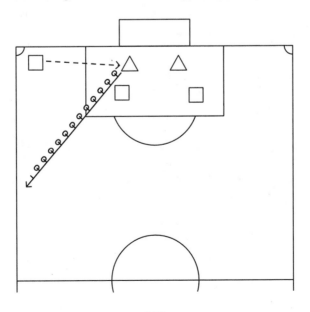

192. DEFENDERS RECOVERING GOAL-SIDE OF THE BALL WHEN OPPONENTS HAVE BEATEN THEM

Organization:

Two defenders and two attackers.

Purpose:

To practice recovering goal-side of the ball as quickly as possible when defenders are beaten by an attacker

Procedure:

Defender A allows attacker D to dribble past. Defender B must now move across to jockey and tackle player D, while defender A recovers goal-side of the ball as quickly as possible and watches attacker E approaching. As soon as attacker D dribbles past defender A, the game is live and attackers D and E must try to beat defenders A and B to score a goal.

Coaching points:

Defender B left his or her position marking attacker E in order to cover for defender A who was beaten by attacker D. Although defender A must now recover toward the center of the field to take defender B's position, the first concern of defender A must be to recover goal-side of the ball in case defender B should be beaten by attacker D, at which time defender A will have to attempt to tackle attacker D again. Defender A must also cover and watch attacker E in case attacker D passes the ball to E.

©2001 by Prentice Hall

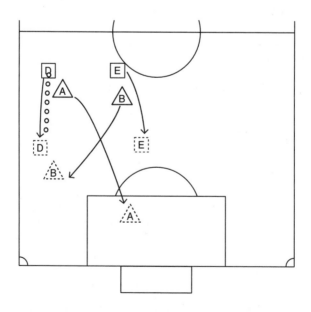

193. MAN-TO-MAN AND ZONE DEFENSE

Organization:

A regular scrimmage game.

Purpose:

To practice both man-to-man marking and zone marking

To learn when each method is appropriate

Procedure:

A regular scrimmage game is played, except the forwards from both teams are instructed to switch positions—left, right, and center—as much as possible during the game. They should do this both when the ball is close by in the attacking third of the field, and when the play is not near them at all; this is so the defenses can practice using both zone and man-to-man marking.

Coaching points:

Defenders must mark man-to-man and stick with their opponent when the play is close to the goal they are defending. Switching opponents with teammates as they move around near the goal can give attackers an extra yard and split second to control the ball and shoot or pass into the penalty area, which may result in a goal. Defenders must mark their opponents tighter the closer they are to goal and the closer the play is to them.

When the play is away from the defensive third of the field, defenders may play zone defense; as an opponent moves away from the left fullback's position, for example, the left fullback should switch the opponent over to a teammate and look for an opponent he or she can mark who is approaching the area. Obviously, good vision and communication between defenders is essential in these situations so each player knows exactly who he or she is marking. When playing this zone defense system, defenders must be very aware of and watch for teammates who are marking two opponents; for example, if the left fullback passes his or her opponents as he or she moves away from the left fullback area, he or she must make sure the defending teammate who will be marking that opponent does not already have a player to mark. If that is the case, the left fullback may have to move with the opponent and play man-to-man marking to avoid having a teammate mark two players.

194. MAN-TO-MAN MARKING

Organization:

A regular game is played, except each player can only tackle one player from the opposing team.

Purpose:

To practice man-to-man marking

Procedure:

Players must mark their opponent closely when the other team is in possession of the ball, and try to lose their opponent when their team has the ball. This drill is also a very good fitness exercise.

Coaching points:

Players must watch the game as well as the player they are marking. When their team has possession of the ball, players must sprint to lose their marker and find space to receive a pass to head toward the goal while avoiding their particular marker.

195. EACH TEAM ATTACKS AND DEFENDS TWO GOALS

Organization:
The field is set up using one half of the field with four goals.

Purpose:
To emphasize all players must use good vision, by having attackers switch their attack from one goal to the other, and defenders reading this switch and covering all players

Procedure:
Both teams must look for and use space when attacking, which can be achieved by suddenly switching the attack from one goal to the next. Defenders must cover both goals. Although they should be closer to the goal the opposing team is attacking at that moment, they must be aware of opposing players at the other goals in case the attacking play is suddenly switched to that goal.

Coaching points:
Sweepers should benefit greatly from this drill, since they are in effect covering two goals at once. Although all defenders must read and be aware of how the play may change and where opposing players are positioned, the sweeper should be verbal in communicating with and organizing the rest of the defense. Defenders must understand how to split two attackers and mark them both simultaneously; this means standing closer to the one who is closer to the ball and the play, while at the same time dropping off far enough goal-side of the other player so should the ball be passed to this player, the defender will have time and space to recover and mark that player closely.

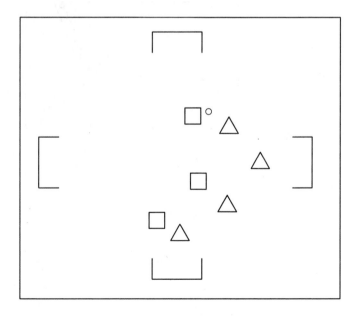

196. SCORE A GOAL BY CROSSING THE ENDLINE

Organization:
A field is set up with no goals.

Purpose:
To encourage defenders to know where all attackers are positioned and to mark them goal-side

Procedure:
A regular game is played except there are no goals and players can only score by dribbling the ball under control across the endline they are attacking.

Coaching points:
This drill encourages the attackers on both teams to spread out and use the full width of the field. Defenders must accommodate for this and make sure they cover all players goal-side of the ball and do not allow them to dribble to the endline. The midfield on both sides must be sure to track back and help the defense, since if the attackers outnumber the defense, the attack should be able to score by passing the ball to a free player who can dribble unmarked over the endline.

©2001 by Prentice Hall

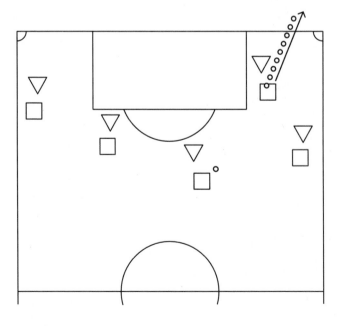

197. PRACTICE DEFENDING AGAINST CROSSED BALLS

Organization:

A regular game is played except that a 5-yard area is coned off along the length of either sideline where no one may enter except the two players already there.

Purpose:

To create a drill where a lot of crosses are kicked into the penalty box

Procedure:

The two players in the marked-off sideline areas play for both teams. When a team wins possession of the ball, it must attempt to pass it to one of these two players as quickly as possible. These players will then run toward the endline of the attacking goal of the team in possession of the ball and cross the ball into the penalty box. The defending team at this goal must clear the ball away from danger, and preferably to one of the wide players in the marked-off zone, who then dribbles with the ball toward the endline at the other goal to cross the ball into that penalty box for the team now attacking.

Coaching points:

Clearances by the defense should be high and wide so they do not simply land just outside the penalty box for an attacker to shoot the ball straight back at goal. Attacks and counterattacks should be carried out at speed, so midfielders and attackers must recover to their half of the field quickly, and the defense that initiated the attack must push up quickly to the halfway line.

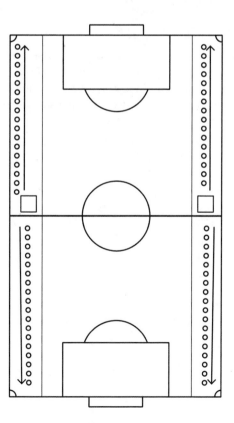

198. READING AND INTERCEPTING ATTACKING THROUGH BALLS

Organization:

A regular game is played, but with small goals, smaller penalty boxes, and no goal-keepers. Defenders cannot enter their own penalty box.

Purpose:

To ensure defenders do not "ball watch," but rather watch the player they are marking as well as the ball

Procedure:

Attackers may score by either dribbling the ball into the penalty area and shooting between the cones or passing the ball into the penalty area at the same time a teammate makes a run there. Defenders may not enter their own penalty box. This means they must mark their opponents very closely and goal-side, and must also watch to make sure opponents do not make a run goal-side of them to receive a pass inside or near the penalty area.

Coaching points:

Defenders must make sure they stay with their opponents and are always goal-side of them as well as the ball. If their player moves to another position, they must make sure they continue to mark closely and only pass them to a teammate if there is time to do so. Man-to-man marking should be used in front of goal and the penalty box.

©2001 by Prentice Hall

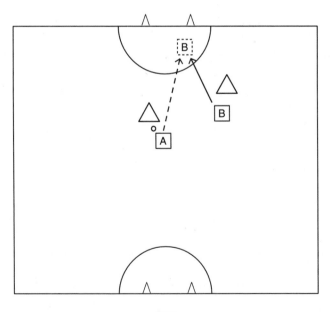

199. CROSSING THE BALL AND SHOOTING

Organization:

Players form 3 lines at the halfway line facing goal and goalie. As the 1st line A player runs down the sideline to cross the ball, 1st B and C players run to penalty area to receive the cross.

Purpose:

To practice crossing the ball; to practice scoring goals from these crosses

Procedure:

Player from line A dribbles around cones, runs to endline, and crosses the ball to the penalty area. Crossed balls should be to the near post, or toward the penalty area and far post, and should be driven or floated. The players from lines B and C must time their runs into the penalty area so they arrive at the same time as the ball.

Coaching points:

Low hard crosses are effective when kicked toward the nearpost where a touch with the foot or head can redirect the ball into the goal. Play high floated crosses toward the farpost since goalkeepers—backpedaling to the ball—must decide whether to leave their line to come for the ball. Attacking players should time their runs to run and jump to head the ball front on to give their shots maximum power.

Players should take the ball to the endline before crossing it since the ball will be coming back toward attackers running toward the goal. This enables attackers to head the ball harder as they meet the ball front on and also makes the cross harder for the goalie to catch since the ball is traveling away from them. If players crossing the ball from the left cross with their left foot (or a right-footed cross from the right), the ball should also naturally curve back toward their forward-moving teammates, making the cross even more difficult for the goalie to save.

Although we think of crosses as goal-scoring opportunities with the head, players must be able to score in any way with any other body part besides arms or hands. Remind players they will have little time in the penalty box since opponents are marking them closely, so they must be alert and on the balls of their feet to move to meet the ball and be first to put a slight touch on it—often all that is required—to redirect it into the goal.

Defenders may be introduced after the attackers have mastered the drill.

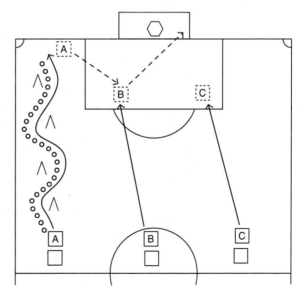

200. CROSSES PULLED BACK TO THE EDGE
OF THE PENALTY BOX

Organization:

One attacker dribbles the ball down the wing and pulls back the cross to a teammate who is running from midfield toward the edge of the penalty box.

Purpose:

To practice pulling the ball back to the edge of the box for a teammate to shoot on goal when the opposing team expects a cross toward the goal

Procedure:

As the attacking wide player reaches the endline and crosses the ball, instead of crossing the ball to the heads of the attackers near the goal, the ball is pulled back along the ground for a midfielder timing a run toward the edge of the penalty box. This move can be very effective, since most defenders will be running back toward their goal when the ball is suddenly played away from the direction in which they are running, thus giving the striker an extra split second when taking the shot.

©2001 by Prentice Hall

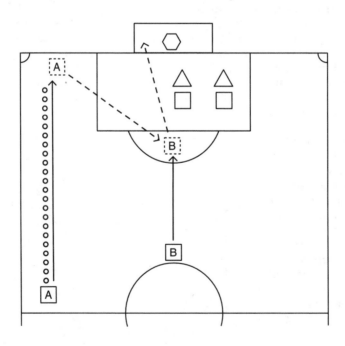

201. DRIBBLE AND PASS

Organization:

Three attackers play against two defenders.

Purpose:

To teach players to draw and beat an opponent to create space

Procedure:

The attacker with the ball dribbles toward a space and the goal to draw a defender. As the defender approaches, the attacker should look for a free teammate (since there are only two defenders, it means one is closing down the player with the ball, one should be marking one of the other two attackers, and the third attacker will be free). The pass should be to the free teammate if possible; if this is not possible, the attacker with the ball should attempt to dribble past the defender and then look to pass, or possibly shoot on goal if in a good position to do so.

Coaching points:

Attackers must realize if they run toward space, it can draw the defender away from marking another player. This creates space since the defender leaves one player and moves to contend with the player in possession of the ball. The player with the ball should then look to pass to the free player in space, or beat the defender and then pass.

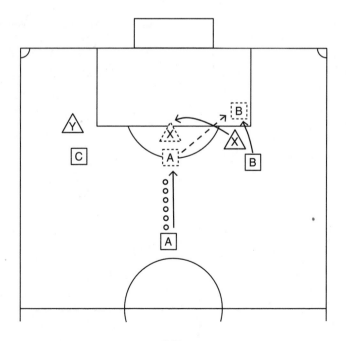

202. CREATING SPACE AND DEPTH IN THE ATTACK

Organization:

Defense versus attack, using half the field.

Purpose:

To help attacking players spread out widthwise and lengthwise so they are never in a flat line across the field.

Procedure:

The attacking team must try to score goals, while the defense simply needs to clear or pass the ball up to the halfway line, at which time the drill starts again. Attackers must make sure they are never in a flat line across the field, since the player in possession will have great difficulty passing to them, and the defense will have little difficulty in marking them. Instead, attacking players must move for each other off the ball so as to create passing angles and space. If players support their teammates on the ball by moving toward them, this not only creates a passing angle but also opens up a space in the position that they moved from, into which another teammate can move and create a further passing option. Therefore, when a player is in possession of the ball, some players should support by moving toward the ball, some by moving away from the ball, some by moving forward, and some by moving backward. Even when players move to support a teammate, but have defenders marking them so closely that they cannot receive the ball, it does not mean that their supporting effort has been in vain; quite to the contrary, they have drawn a defender out of position so another supporting run can be made into the area the space that has been created.

©2001 by Prentice Hall

Coaching points:

Attackers should bring the ball forward down the wings as much as possible; this not only spreads the attack and opens the opposing defense as much as possible, but there is more room for forwards to dribble and use their skills on the wings. Then, when the ball is in the attacking third of the field, it can be crossed or passed into the central area of the field toward the penalty area in order to create goal-scoring opportunities. Attackers should never be afraid to pass the ball backward if there are no opportunities going forward; it is far better to keep possession of the ball and pass it backward, than to attempt to go forward in a no-hope situation.

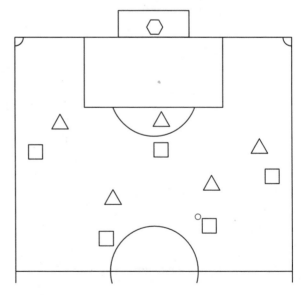

203. DIAGONAL PENETRATING PASSES TO BEAT THE OFFSIDE TRAP

Organization:

Defense versus attack, using half the field.

Purpose:

To help attacking players beat the offside trap

Procedure:

The defense plays the offside trap by positioning themselves in a flat line across the field. The attackers penetrate the offside trap by making well-timed diagonal runs onto passes played through the defensive line. Player A makes a diagonal run through the defensive line to receive a pass from C.

Coaching points:

Players must remember that if they move behind the defenders after the pass is made, they will not be offside. Players must communicate well to carry out moves like this.

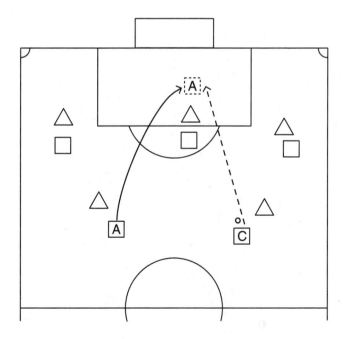

204. SPREADING OUT AND CREATING SPACE

Organization:

A regular scrimmage game.

Purpose:

To help players spread out

Procedure:

All passes must be at least 10 yards or more.

Coaching points:

This encourages players to both look for space and find passing angles to receive the ball. This is a particularly good drill to use before playing a real game on a very wide field, so players will have practiced and are used to taking advantage of the width of the field.

©2001 by Prentice Hall

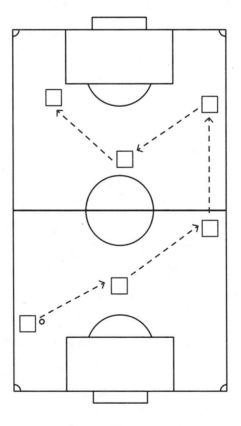

205. CREATING PASSING ANGLES

Organization:

Two defenders are positioned in a central grid between two sets of two attackers, with each set in its own grid to either side of them.

Purpose:

To teach attackers how to create passing angles for players wishing to pass the ball to them

Procedure:

None of the players may leave their respective grids. The two pairs of attackers must attempt to pass the ball to each other through the central grid containing the two defenders. The attackers without the ball must keep moving to create passing angles to receive the ball. Attackers within the same grid can also pass to each other, in order to draw the defense away from the position they are holding to prevent the through passes.

Coaching points:

Attackers must communicate well with one another, not only verbally, but also by using such methods as eye contact, whereby players with the ball can read where their teammates will move to receive the ball by the way they quickly look toward an open space and then move toward it as they anticipate the pass.

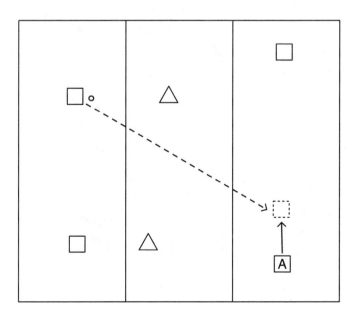

206. FAKES AND DRIBBLING MOVES THAT CAN BE USED TO GET PAST OPPONENTS

Organization:

Players inside a grid with their own ball.

Purpose:

To practice dribbling and performing the many fakes that can be used to beat opponents

Procedure:

Players dribble around inside the grid and perform fakes as they approach other players also dribbling around.

Coaching points:

Players must keep their heads up so they can avoid contact with other players, and so they can continuously look for new spaces to head toward. Although there are no opponents challenging for the ball in this drill, players must use this opportunity to practice the various different fakes they have learned, and must practice them at speed, just as in a real game.

207. FOUR VERSUS ONE AROUND A GRID

Organization:

Four players stand along the four sides of a grid with one opponent in the middle.

Purpose:

To practice creating good passing angles for teammates

Procedure:

The players along the four sides of the grid must move from side to side along their respective sidelines in order to pass the ball between themselves, and to prevent the defender from winning the ball by tackling or intercepting it.

Coaching points:

This drill helps players understand that supporting their teammates means not only finding a space in which to receive the ball, but also being in a position where their teammate can pass to them. If player A has the ball, players B and C must move along their lines toward the line where A is positioned, so they can create passing angles for A to pass the ball to either of them. It is important that the player with the ball (player A in this example) always has at least two passing options (to players B and C in this example), since if there is only one passing option, the defender will know where the pass will be going.

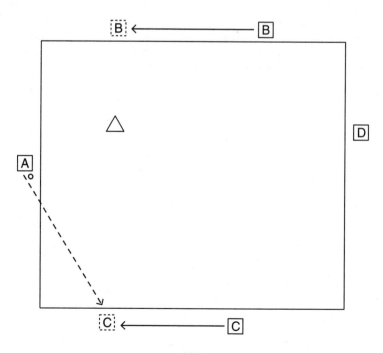

208. PREPARING QUICKLY FOR FREE KICKS AND CORNER KICKS

Organization:

A regular scrimmage game is played, except the coach can blow the whistle at any time and award a free kick or corner kick to either team.

Purpose:

To practice organizing as quickly as possible at corners and free kicks

To practice defending and attacking at such set pieces

Procedure:

The coach blows the whistle at any time during the scrimmage and awards a free kick or corner kick to either team, even though a foul may not have been committed or the ball may not have traveled out of bounds. The team awarded the kick must collect the ball as quickly as possible and take the kick, while the defending team must recover goal-side of the ball as quickly as possible and position themselves to defend against the kick.

Coaching points:

Attackers and defenders must know where they must stand and what their particular duties are at corners and free kicks. Attackers will quite often want to take the kick as quickly as possible in order to catch defenders offguard, while defenders will want to arrange and organize themselves as quickly as possible to prevent this. However, although attackers will often wish to take free kicks and corners quickly, there will be times when the referee instructs them that they must wait for the whistle before kicking the ball. Whichever the case, attackers must be sure to take advantage of the free kick or corner kick, since they represent excellent goal-scoring opportunities.

Section 10

FITNESS DRILLS

Section 10

FITNESS DRILLS

Add a competitive edge to the fitness drills described in this section by either having players compete against each other or by dividing the players into two lines/groups that compete against each other.

Many of the warm-up drills described in Section 1, and many of the drills described in the sections throughout this book, can be used as fitness drills simply by performing more repetitions and performing the drills at a quicker pace.

209. RUNNING

Running is an excellent way of getting and staying fit. Players should vary the length of their runs and also the speed at which they run. A long run is good for building stamina, while a shorter/faster run, with sprints and other exercises possibly included, will help build speed and strength.

210. TO THE FRONT

Players form a line one behind the other and run along with about three yards between each person. When the coach blows the whistle, the last player in the line sprints to the front of the line, so each player runs from the back to the front at least once.

211. TO THE BACK OF THE LINE

Players form a line one behind the other and run along with about three yards between each person. When the coach blows the whistle, the front player turns and sprints to the back of the line, so each player runs from the front to the back at least once.

212. BACKWARD TO THE BACK

Players form a line one behind the other and run along with about three yards between each person. When the coach blows the whistle, the front player runs quickly backward to the back of the line, so each player runs from the front of the line to the back at least once.

213. WEAVING TO THE FRONT

Players form a line one behind the other and run along with about three yards between each person. When the coach blows the whistle, the back player runs to the front of the line by weaving between the other players, so each player weaves from the back of the line to the front at least once.

214. WEAVING TO THE BACK

Players form a line one behind the other and run along with about three yards between each player. When the coach blows the whistle, the front player turns and weaves between the other players to the back of the line, so each player weaves from the front to the back of the line at least once.

215. JOG AND SPRINT AROUND THE FIELD

Players form a line one behind the other with about three yards between each person. Players jog slowly around the soccer field. When the coach blows the whistle, the front player sprints on ahead around the soccer field until he or she reaches the back of the line.

216. LEAPFROG

Players stand in a line one behind the other with about three yards between each person. The back player leapfrogs over all the players in front, who must bend over with their hands resting on their thighs. As soon as the back player has leapfrogged over two or three people, the new back person begins, so that the line continuously moves forward.

217. SHUTTLES TO CONES

Players line up behind a cone with three more cones 10 yards apart in a line in front of them. The first player sprints from the first cone to the second cone and back to the first cone, then to the third cone and back to the first cone, then to the fourth cone and back to the first cone, before the next player performs the same drill.

218. SPRINT AND SIT

Players line up behind one cone, with another cone 10 yards in front of them. The first player sprints to the cone 10 yards away, performs 10 push-ups (or sit-ups, star-jumps, squat thrusts), and then runs back to the start to tag the next person who performs the same exercise.

219. SPRINT FORWARD AND BACKWARD

Players line up behind one cone, with another cone 10 yards in front of them. The front player sprints forward to the cone 10 yards away and then sprints backward to the start, where they tag the next player.

220. TOUCH THE COACH'S FOOT

Players form a circle around the coach, who stands in the middle about 5 to 10 yards away from each player. One player starts the drill by running to and touching the coach's foot, then running to touch the next player's foot (the next player in a counterclockwise direction), then running to touch the coach's foot again, then running to touch the next player's foot, and so on, until the player arrives back to the original position. After this player has touched two or three other players' feet, the next player should begin the same drill and should try to catch up with the player in front before this player gets back to the starting position.

221. SPRINT AND JUMP

Players line up one behind the other. The first player sprints five yards and lies down sideways on the ground. The second player sprints and jumps over the first player lying on the floor, runs another five yards, and lies down also. The third player sprints and jumps over the first two players and then also lies down five yards further on. When the last player in the line has sprinted, jumped over all the players lying down, and laid down, the first player gets up again and sprints forward over all the players lying down, and lies down again, and so on.

222. CHANGING SPEEDS

Players line up side by side about three yards apart and jog forward. When the coach blows the whistle, the players sprint until the coach blows the whistle again to indicate players jog again. Players need to practice changing pace in this way from a slow jog to a fast sprint, since this skill can be very effective in games for beating and losing opponents.

223. JUMP OVER THE BALL

Players stand with their legs together beside a soccer ball. When the coach blows the whistle, players jump sideways over the ball with their feet together from one side to the other for a given period of time or until a certain number of repetitions have been completed. Players should also perform this drill jumping backward and forward over the ball with their feet together.

224. LIFT AND HOLD

Players lie down with their backs on the ground. The coach instructs players to lift both feet 6 to 12 inches off the ground, and hold them in that position. After 10 or 20 seconds, players are instructed to part their legs, while keeping the raised feet at the same height above the ground. Coaches then proceed to instruct players to move their feet to different positions after 10 to 20 seconds, all the time without resting the feet. Such movements could include crisscrossing the legs and the feet from one side to the other, or placing the feet together and moving them around in a circular motion. Players of different strengths, ages, and abilities will obviously perform this exercise for different lengths of time.

225. PIGGYBACK

Players line up behind one cone, with another cone 10 yards in front of them. Players pair off with partners of similar weight and height. Players run to the cone 10 yards in front of them while giving their partner a piggyback ride, and then run back to the start before the next pair begins.

226. KNEES UP

Players jump on a spot and bring both knees together up to their chest 10 times.

227. KICK UP YOUR HEELS

Players stand on the spot and kick their heels up behind them for a certain time period or for a number of repetitions.

228. TEAM SPRINTS

Players arrange themselves into groups of three. One player stands by a cone facing two other players standing by a cone 10 yards away. The first player from the group of two sprints toward the player 10 yards away and tags that player. That player then sprints back toward the player opposite so this player can then perform the 10-yard sprint, and so on, until each player has completed a certain number of 10-yard sprints.

229. CALISTHENICS

Performing press-ups, sit-ups, and star-jumps are excellent ways to achieve and maintain fitness. Players should either perform a certain number of these exercises or perform as many as possible in a given time period.

230. WHEELBARROW RACES

Players stand in pairs with one player holding the second player's legs so the second player moves over a given distance using the arms.

231. JUMP UP AND BACK

Players jump forward with both feet together and then backward in the same way.

232. SPRINT AND CHASE ON DEMAND

Players stand in a circular formation. The coach calls out a player's name to indicate this player must sprint around the outside of the circle in a counterclockwise direction and back to the original position. A split second after this player starts sprinting, the coach will blow the whistle to indicate that the player to the left of the player who is already running must chase this player and try to catch him or her.

233. BUNNY HOPS

Players crouch down and place their hands on their knees so they can move by bouncing forward with both legs while remaining in the crouched position.

234. SPRINT, SIT, UP, AND SPRINT

Players sprint forward. Each time the coach blows the whistle, players must sit down, get up again as quickly as possible, and resume running.

235. SPRINT, LIE, UP, AND RUN

Players run forward. Each time the coach blows the whistle, players must lie down, get up again as quickly as possible, and resume running.

236. RUN, SIT-UPS, RESUME

Players run forward. Each time the coach blows the whistle, players must perform five push-ups/sit-ups as quickly as possible, and then resume running.

237. SPRINT RACES

Players race against each other or against the clock over distances ranging from 50 yards to 400 yards.

238. SPRINT THEN JOG IN PLACE

Players sprint in place for 30 seconds, jog in place for 30 seconds, sprint on the spot again for 30 seconds, and so on. It is important that players have good stamina to play soccer; being able to recover from a sprint while jogging is essential.

239. SPRINT AND TURN

Players sprint forward. When the coach blows the whistle, players turn and sprint the other way, and so on.

240. SPRINT AND TURN AROUND

Players sprint forward. When the coach blows the whistle, players turn 360 degrees and continue sprinting.

241. LEAPFROG AND CRAWL

Players stand in a line one behind the other with about three yards between each person. The back player leapfrogs the first player in front, who must bend over with his or her hands resting on his or her thighs and then crawls through the legs of the next player and so on. As soon as the back player has leapfrogged over one or two people, the new back person begins, so the line continuously moves forward.

242. SPRINT AND CHASE

One player sprints forward. When the coach blows the whistle, the next player sprints forward and tries to catch the first player, and so on.

243. HILL SPRINTS

Players sprint up the hill and jog back down.

244. IMAGINARY BIKE

Players lie on their backs with their legs in the air and ride an imaginary bike. When the coach blows the whistle, players pedal fast; when the coach blows the whistle again, they slow down, and so on.

245. FEET UP

Players are in pairs. One player lies on his or her back and holds onto the ankles of the other player who stands by the supine player's shoulders. The players lying down keep their legs straight and raise them up to the hands of the standing players. The standing players grab the feet and push them back toward the ground. The players lying down must keep their feet/legs from touching the ground.

246. HOLD THEM BACK

Players find a partner of equal or close weight and height. One partner stands behind the other. The front player runs forward while the back player attempts to prevent the front player from doing so by holding the front player around the waist.

247. TUG OF WAR

Players find a partner of equal or close weight and height. The two players face each other, hold each other's hands, and move backward while trying to pull the opponent forward.

248. OVER THE ROPE

A rope is tied between the goal posts two feet from the ground. Players must jump from side to side with both feet together 20 times. The rope can be raised or lowered as necessary.

249. JUMP ROPE

Players each have a jump rope and must either perform a set number of jumps or jump for a set length of time.

250. RING AROUND THE PENALTY BOX

Players form a line one behind the other and run around the penalty box. Players jog the lengths and sprint the widths.

251. JOG AND SPRINT AROUND THE PENALTY BOX

Players form a line one behind the other and run around the penalty box. Players jog one length, then sprint one width, then jog one length, sprint one width and one length, then jog one width, then sprint one length and one width and one more length, and so on, so the pattern is jog one sprint one, jog one sprint two, jog one sprint three.

Section 11

THE RULES OF SOCCER

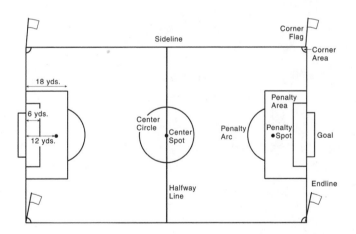

Section 11
THE RULES OF SOCCER

As with most other sports, referees enforce the rules needed to ensure the game of soccer is organized, safe, and fun. Although FIFA (Federation Internationale de Football Association) sets the rules used in soccer worldwide, different organizations, such as high school and college soccer organizations, modify these rules slightly; however, they still all conform to the basic FIFA laws. This section will outline a basic set of rules.

The Field of Play

The soccer field is rectangular shaped and varies in size according to the age and number of players. For example, a suitable field size for players ages 12 and up would be up to the maximum of 60 yards wide and 110 yards long, while for players ages 9–11, it would be between 35–45 yards wide and 50–70 yards long. The diagram of the field below shows how a soccer field would officially be lined out.

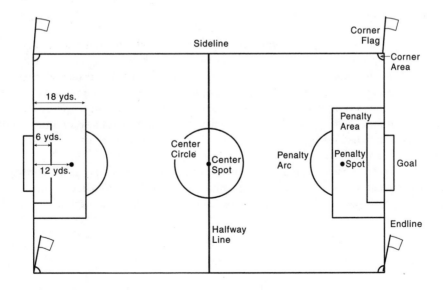

The Ball

The ball should be size 5 for players ages 12 and up, size 3 for players up to the age of 7, and size 4 for players ages 8–11.

The Players

At age 12 and older, each team will have a maximum of 11 players and play on a full-size soccer field with full-size goals. Younger players who play on a smaller field will usually have five, six, seven, or eight players on the field at any time.

Uniform

A team will wear uniforms of the same color (except for the goalkeeper), and the color must be clearly different from the uniform of the opposing team. Players are not allowed to wear dangerous or sharp objects such as watches, jewelry, or shoes with sharp cleats.

The Referee and Linesmen

A game may have one referee and two linesmen as officials. The linesmen indicate only out-of-bounds, offsides, and incidents off the ball. The referee has the final say in any decision. Recreational soccer games, played for fun, will usually use just one official, the referee.

Start of Play

A coin toss before the game—with the two captains attending and one calling it—decides who gets either to take the kickoff or the end at which his or her team will start (the sun and direction of the wind usually affect this decision). The team that loses the coin toss decides the remaining choice. The opposing team must be in its own half of the field at the start of play and outside the center circle. The ball must go forward one full revolution to start play and the kicker may not touch the ball a second time until it has been touched by any other player on the field. The game is also started in this manner after a goal, with the team scored against taking the kickoff.

If the referee has to stop the game and neither team is entitled to take the restart, the game shall be restarted with a dropball; two players, one from each team, stand face-to-face, the referee drops the ball between them, and the game starts after the ball touches the ground.

The Ball Out-of-Bounds

The entire ball must cross the endline or sideline for it to be out of play. If only part of the ball touches or crosses the line, it is still in play.

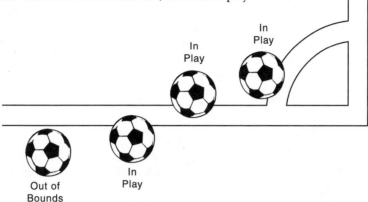

Scoring Goals

The team that has scored more goals at the end of the game wins. A goal is scored when the whole ball crosses over the goal line, and may be scored with any part of the body except the arm or hand.

Throw-ins

A throw-in is used to restart the game after the ball has traveled over either sideline, and is awarded to the team that did not touch the ball last. The thrower must stand behind the line and keep both feet on the ground when throwing the ball. When throwing, players throw the ball using both hands, and by bringing the ball from behind the neck and releasing it above and over the head. The throw-in is taken from the point where the ball crossed the line. The thrower may not touch the ball after it has been thrown in until another player on the field has touched it. The penalty for performing a throw-in incorrectly is the award of the throw-in to the other team.

Goal Kicks

A goal kick is awarded when the ball goes out-of-bounds across the endline and was last touched by the team attacking the goal at that end of the field. The kick is taken from the corner of the 6-yard box on the side of the goal that the ball passed the end-line. Any player may take the goal kick, but the ball must go out of the penalty area before another player can touch it. If this rule is infringed, the kick is taken again.

The goal kick is an indirect kick (see Fouls and Free Kicks), which means that a goal cannot be scored from a goal kick without another player touching the ball first.

Corner Kicks

A corner kick is awarded when the ball goes out-of-bounds across the endline and was last touched by the team defending that goal. The corner kick is taken from within the quarter circle at the corner on the side nearest where the ball traveled past the endline. The defending team must stand at least 10 yards from the ball when it is kicked.

The corner kick is a direct kick, which means the kicker can score a goal directly without another player touching the ball. Just as with the throw-in, the kicker cannot touch the ball a second time until it has touched another player.

Penalty Kicks

A penalty kick is awarded to the attacking team if the defending team gives up a direct free kick inside the penalty area. The penalty kick is a free kick at goal by a designated player against only the goalkeeper. All other players must remain outside the penalty area and arc. Goalkeepers must stand on the goal line, and may not move sideways* until the ball has been kicked.

The ball may not be played a second time by the kicker until the ball has been touched by another player and play continues as normal should the goalkeeper save the kick. If the defending team violates a rule (for example, by entering the penalty area before the ball has been kicked), the kick is retaken if a goal is not scored. If the attacking team infringes a rule, the kick is retaken if a goal is scored, but play is continued if no goal is scored. If a penalty kick is taken at the end of a half or the end of the game, no second attempt at scoring is allowed if the goalkeeper saves the ball and deflects it back into the playing area.

©2001 by Prentice Hall

Fouls and Free Kicks

In soccer, players may not push, trip, kick, or hold an opposing player, and they may not deliberately use their hands or arms to touch or control the ball. Any of these infringements will result in a free kick being awarded to the other team. A free kick can be either in the form of a direct free kick or an indirect free kick. A goal can be scored directly from a direct free kick, while the ball must touch another player before going into the goal from an indirect free kick.

A direct free kick will be the result of kicking, tripping, holding, pushing, or handling the ball. An indirect free kick will be the result of offside, obstruction, the goalkeeper picking up the ball from a backpass, or the goalkeeper taking more than six seconds* to distribute the ball.

Referees will hold an arm straight up in the air to indicate to players that the free kick is an indirect free kick, and will make no signal other than blowing the whistle and pointing to the spot where the kick is to be taken for a direct free kick. Players may also ask the referee if the kick is direct or indirect, but it is better that players

---

*New rule in 2000.

know the signals in case the attacking team takes the free kick quickly and the defending team is not properly prepared.

When a free kick is taken, the opposing team must be at least 10 yards from the ball. If the kick is being taken from inside the penalty area by the defending team, the ball must travel outside the penalty area before being touched by another player. If the ball is awarded to the attacking team inside the penalty area in the form of an indirect free kick and the ball is less than 10 yards from the goal line, defending team members are permitted to stand on the goal line, even though this may be less than 10 yards from the ball.

If players deliberately foul or play dangerously in soccer, the referee may give them a yellow card for the first offense (which is a warning), and a red card the next time a bad foul is committed (which means the player must leave the game). For very dangerous fouls a red card can be issued with no prior yellow card having been given.

Offside

Offside results in an indirect free kick being awarded to the opposing team, and is a rule to prevent attackers from simply waiting at the goal for goal-scoring opportunities. Players are offside if, when the ball is passed forward to them, they do not have two players (including the goalkeeper) between them and the goal line. Players cannot be offside in their own half of the field; directly from a throw-in, a corner kick, a goal kick; or if they are not interfering with the play or an opponent. Players are also not offside if they are in line with, but not in front of, the last defender.

Goalkeeper Steps and Handling Rules

Goalkeepers may handle the ball only inside the penalty area. Once they have the ball in their hands, they must distribute the ball within 6 seconds. If a team plays the ball to its own goalkeeper, the goalkeeper may not pick up the ball unless it was received by a header or an unintentional back pass.* Any infringements on these rules will result in an indirect free kick to the opposing team.

©2001 by Prentice Hall

---

*New rule: The goalkeeper may no longer pick up a ball received by a throw-in.

FIVE
EASY-TO-FOLLOW
PRACTICE SESSIONS

Section 12

FIVE EASY-TO-FOLLOW
PRACTICE SESSIONS

This section describes five easy-to-follow practice sessions formulated by combining various drills and exercises from the book. Four are designed for field players and one is designed for goalkeepers. All five sessions should illustrate how easily many more similar sessions can be devised by using this book and the blank table at the end of this section, which can be photocopied as many times as you need it for your team and your own planning purposes.

PRACTICE SESSION 1

TYPE OF SKILL	DRILL #	PAGE #	TIME TO BE SPENT ON DRILL IN MINUTES
Warming up	1	5	
Warming up	7	6	
Warming up	8	6	
Warming up	10	7	
Warming up	11	7	
Warming up	13	7	10–15
Stretching	33	11	
Stretching	35	12	
Stretching	40	12	
Stretching	47	14	
Stretching	37	12	
Dribbling	113	86	
Dribbling	114	87	
Dribbling	115	88	
Dribbling	116	89	15
Dribbling	117	90	
Dribbling	123	96	
Passing	61	22	10
Shooting	90	51	
Tackling	128	101	10
Tackling	129	108	
Scrimmage	188	190	20

PRACTICE SESSION 2

TYPE OF SKILL	DRILL #	PAGE #	TIME TO BE SPENT ON DRILL IN MINUTES
Warming up	1	5	
Warming up	6	6	
Warming up	7	6	
Warming up	8	6	
Warming up	10	7	
Warming up	13	7	
Stretching	33	11	10–15
Stretching	38	12	
Stretching	39	12	
Stretching	41	13	
Stretching	37	12	
Stretching	34	11	
Stretching	35	12	
Stretching	40	12	
Dribbling	112	85	
Dribbling	113	86	
Dribbling	114	87	15
Dribbling	115	88	
Dribbling	117	90	
Dribbling	120	93	
Passing	61	22	
Passing	62	23	10
Juggling	2	5	5
Tackling	135	114	10
Scrimmage	188	190	20

PRACTICE SESSION 3

TYPE OF SKILL	DRILL #	PAGE #	TIME TO BE SPENT ON DRILL IN MINUTES
Warming up	1	5	
Warming up	6	6	
Warming up	7	6	
Warming up	12	7	
Warming up	14	7	
Warming up	15	8	
Stretching	42	13	10–15
Stretching	33	11	
Stretching	34	11	
Stretching	35	12	
Stretching	40	12	
Stretching	45	13	
Stretching	37	12	
Stretching	46	14	
Dribbling	110	83	
Dribbling	111	84	15
Dribbling	121	94	
Shooting	80	41	15
Throw-ins	140	123	10
Throw-ins	141	124	
Scrimmage	188	190	20

PRACTICE SESSION 4

TYPE OF SKILL	DRILL #	PAGE #	TIME TO BE SPENT ON DRILL IN MINUTES
Warming up	1	5	
Warming up	16	8	
Warming up	11	7	
Warming up	12	7	
Stretching	33	11	
Stretching	34	11	10–15
Stretching	35	12	
Stretching	40	12	
Stretching	43	13	
Stretching	44	13	
Stretching	38	12	
Dribbling	112	85	
Dribbling	124	97	15
Trapping	97	65	
Trapping	99	67	
Trapping	100	68	20
Trapping	105	73	
Scrimmage	188	190	20

PRACTICE SESSION 5 (GOALKEEPING)

TYPE OF SKILL	DRILL #	PAGE #	TIME TO BE SPENT ON DRILL IN MINUTES
Warming up	1	5	
Warming up	3	5	
Warming up	4	6	
Warming up	6	6	
Warming up	7	6	
Warming up	8	6	
Warming up	10	7	
Stretching	33	11	
Stretching	34	11	
Stretching	35	12	10–15
Stretching	36	12	
Stretching	37	12	
Stretching	38	12	
Stretching	42	13	
Stretching	43	13	
Stretching	44	13	
Stretching	45	13	
Stretching	46	14	
Stretching	47	14	
Goalkeeping	157	145	
Goalkeeping	160	156	
Goalkeeping	162	158	50
Goalkeeping	166	162	
Goalkeeping	169	165	
Goalkeeping	170	166	

PRACTICE SESSION TABLE

TYPE OF SKILL	DRILL #	PAGE #	TIME TO BE SPENT ON DRILL IN MINUTES